GODDESS SPIRITUALITY
FOR THE 21ST CENTURY

GODDESS SPIRITUALITY FOR THE 21ST CENTURY
FROM KABBALAH TO QUANTUM PHYSICS

JUDITH LAURA

Triangle Books

Triangle Books
are published by
Research Triangle Publishing, Inc.
PO Box 1130
Fuquay-Varina, NC 27526

ISBN 1-884570-64-x

The Bible Scripture quotations in this publication are from The Authorized
King Jame Version except as otherwise noted.

Cover Design by Kathy Holbrook

Library of Congress Catalog Card Number: 97-65320

Printed in the United States of America
10 9 8 7 6 5 4 3 2 1

Table of Contents

Meditations and Rituals

Introduction

↩ A VIBRANT NEW form of spirituality emerged in the last quarter of the twentieth century. Variously known as women's spirituality, feminist theology, and Goddess spirituality, it was born of mid-century feminism. From a few people, scattered across the country, musing privately over the possibility of divinity imaged as female, it grew to a spiritual movement replete with traditions, rituals, and hundreds of thousands of participants not only in the United States but also in many other countries around the globe.

My involvement began in the mid-1970s, when I wondered if religion, like other social institutions, had been influenced by the patriarchal suppression and devaluation of women. There were then few books even touching on the subject, but in a bookstore specializing in esoteric, old books, I found the works of Helen Diner and Esther Harding.[1] They revealed that worship of deity as female existed—indeed it was virtually universal—not only before Judaism and Christianity, but before even the Greek, Roman, and other pantheons in which goddesses were reduced to serving as the wives or daughters of gods.

This information had, by the late 1980s, become more widely published and elaborated upon by contemporary anthropologists, archaeologists, historians, and theo(a)logians.[2]

Today, for me and many others, what began as a politically motivated intellectual adventure has become a joyful journey through an unfolding form of spirituality that allows greater personal participation and experience of the divine. Early on, most of those participating in this new spirituality were women. Today, however, a growing number of men are recognizing its value to themselves personally, to their families, and to society in general. This spiritual movement encompasses many traditions including Pagan, Christian, and Jewish. It also draws inspiration from Native American, African, and Asian traditions.

Perhaps the greatest influence has been Pagan, including Wiccan traditions, in which are preserved, to a certain extent, what we can imagine to be a prepatriarchal form of spirituality. Though quite diverse in their beliefs and practices, in general these groups worship the Goddess and her son/consort, the God (usually characterized as horned, showing his closeness to nature).[3] Some groups, however, worship exclusively the Goddess in her many aspects and personalities and names.[4] I've observed, however, that just because a group bills itself as Pagan and honors the Goddess doesn't mean that it is automatically free of sexism, particularly in the language used in its rituals and in the group interactions. It seems that some Pagan groups, particularly those that predate the feminist spirituality awakening and whose traditions have remained unchanged by it, may also be burdened by patriarchal customs similar to those plaguing other religions.

Within Christian feminism, at least two movements have emerged: Women-Church and the Re-Imagining Community. Most observers credit liberation theologian Rosemary Radford Ruether with starting the Women-Church movement[5] in the 1980s. Initially a predominantly Catholic and Anglican movement, it asserts that women cannot function as whole spiritual persons and still stay strictly within the church, as it now exists. Women-Church advocates, therefore, that women form an exodus from the church and, still retaining their Christian roots, create their own rituals, traditions, and sacred spaces. In addressing divinity, if any gender is used, it is female. The imagery used to describe divinity is also female. A similar movement, the Re-Imagining Community, began in the early '90s. Headquartered in Minneapolis, the community's mission extends to many areas of church life and belief and involves women and some men from many Protestant denominations. Participants at a conference in Minneapolis in 1994, before they spoke, invoked Sophia as Divine Wisdom personified as female. The conference—and some of the participating clergy—were later denounced by some home churches. Nevertheless, a significant number of laypeople and clergy had served notice to their denominations that continuing to personify divinity as "God, he" would no longer do. By their actions and words they had demonstrated their agreement with Carol Christ[6] and others that degenderizing is at present not sufficient to redress the harm that has been done by thousands of years of exclusive male-god language.

One of the Re-Imagining Community's prayers begins:

Bless Sophia, Spirit of Wisdom and Truth,
we who continue to seek new life and a
new vision for the church.

The efforts are similar but perhaps more fragmented for Jewish women. While writers like Blu Greenberg[7] try to beat a path through the morass of Orthodox laws and customs, those customs remain unchanged, and the women within Orthodoxy, like many Roman Catholic women who still blindly follow the Pope, remain bound—or at least reconciled—to those traditions. Conservative Judaism is a mixed bag, apparently depending on the location of the congregation and the openness of the rabbi to new ways of thinking.   Reconstructionist and Reform Judaism continue to be the most comfortable with adapting their worship forms to accommodate objections to exclusive male-god language as well as the lack of female divine imagery. These groups also are at the forefront of including women as full participants, including women as cantors and rabbis.   The Jewish Renewal Movement, a kind of New Age manifestation in Judaism, seems to be making a particular effort to incorporate what Jewish Renewalists usually refer to as the "feminine divine" or the "female face of God."[8] Yet, even in these groups, for the most part, the implication is that God is still "he," but he has a feminine side or aspect.

In her groundbreaking book, *Standing Again at Sinai*, Judith Plaskow advocates what some might consider revolutionary changes in Jewish thought to enable women to become spiritually empowered while staying within that tradition.

Some Jewish women have formed their own feminist spirituality groups, sometimes within and sometimes outside the synagogue walls.   One source to which such women sometimes turn is the Kabbalah, the mystical tradition of Judaism which, in most forms, contains divine feminine images.   Kabbalah was adopted and adapted by Western mystics (usually of Christian background) who transliterate the Hebrew word (meaning that which is received) as "Qabalah."   Yet anyone delving even just a bit beneath the surface of this tradition soon may be stymied by its patriarchal stereotyping, which extends to conceptions of female divinity.   And thus, even Kabbalah, without further reinterpretation, may become a dead end for those seeking matrifocal equality.

From the evolving forms of feminist spirituality in Pagan, Jewish, and Christian settings, many traditions and practices have emerged—from rituals that begin with casting a circle to women's seders.   Yet, there is, for some, a yearning for additional metaphysical or mystical paths consistent with Goddess spirituality and with contemporary life, including scientific knowledge. This yearning may lead participants to explore other spiritual forms such as "New Age" philosophies, theosophy, gnosticism, and other Western esoteric traditions. These explorers, upon finding in what are touted as modern and open traditions many of the same patriarchal prejudices that persist in traditional religions, may feel they have to choose between further spiritual development and spiritual empowerment. I believe that such a choice is unnecessary, for deeper mystical sources exist within Goddess spirituality, though they are so far largely undeveloped and unfocused.

This book offers two possibilities for beginning to deepen and focus the metaphysical base of Goddess spirituality, while at the same time making this form of spirituality more relevant to out times: One is as old as prehistory, the other as new as today's leaps of scientific faith.

The first, Kabbalah, in both its Jewish and Western esoteric forms, can (and should!) be analyzed anew and reinterpreted in light of our present knowledge of prehistory, Goddess religions—particularly of the Middle East—and patriarchal habits such as gender reversal. Only then can we receive Kabbalah's original meaning and intent—and begin to develop it as an appropriate basis for egalitarian metaphysical thought.

The second is quantum physics and cosmology, whose emerging concepts dovetail with long-held Goddess beliefs, including symbolism and understanding of the divine.

Both these paths lead toward a more fully developed matrifocal mysticism. Complete with guided meditations and rituals, they are a spiritual gift waiting to be opened.

Chapter 1
Concepts of Contemporary Goddess Spirituality

↵ THERE IS NO DOGMA—no one set of beliefs—required of people involved in Goddess spirituality. Indeed the range of beliefs and practices are wide, and hopefully their diversity will continue and perhaps even expand. Yet there are a number of concepts common in contemporary Goddess spirituality which continue to be shared sources of discussion and inspiration. Reviewing these evolving concepts will prepare us for explorations of further mystical possibilities.

INCLUSIVE LANGUAGE

The most basic and commonly shared concept in feminist spirituality is that language used to address or talk about divinity should not exclude women, as has much of the language used in traditional Jewish and Christian Scripture and practice.

Usually the first realization on the path to Goddess spirituality is that using exclusively male pronouns for God excludes women from full participation in religion. The argument that the pronouns "he" or "him," when referring to God, are "generic" has been exposed as false, much in the same way that the male pronoun in the sentence, "The student should always do his homework," is now recognized to exclude women or girls from being included in the mind's eye as students. One of the first ways of "consciousness-raising" in early women's spirituality was to replace the words "God, he" with "God, she." Back then, "God, she" was likely to get a good guffaw from the person defending "God, he" as generic. But it seems that the Goddess now has the last laugh.

In addition to male pronouns to describe divinity, such nouns as "Lord," "King," and "Father" used alone to describe a sole divinity are also considered exclusive. Some scholars and laypeople feel that the word "God," even used without male pronouns, denotes a male (the female term being Goddess). Perhaps such a subconscious recognition underlies some of the uneasiness felt with the term "God, she," for indeed, a god is male, whether initialized with a capital or lowercase letter.

Using words such as "man" and "mankind" to mean humans and humanity (or in current parlance, humankind) are also considered exclusive. In a religious context, particularly offensive are phrases such as "God and Man" and "the Brotherhood of Man."

Some mainstream churches have degenderized hymns and prayers in an attempt to attain inclusiveness. This is certainly preferable to the persistence of male nouns and imagery in other churches (including those billing themselves as metaphysical or New Age!), but many people feel that making the jump to gender neutral language skips a necessary step—that of asserting the female divine in a culture that has been lacking it for thousands of years. Only after incorporating explicitly female terms for divinity and thereby explicitly creating feminine imagery, only after allowing those words and images to become as much part of our spiritual consciousness—and subconscious—as the male words, can we, if we so desire, move toward truly gender neutral language in religion.

Therefore, the first step taken in feminist/women's/Goddess spirituality is to image divinity as female.

SHARED LEADERSHIP

Most Western religions (and some Eastern ones as well) are modeled as hierarchies and based on authoritarian concepts. This is most obvious in the Roman Catholic, Orthodox, and Anglican churches. There are Protestant and Jewish sects whose structures are less hierarchical and which claim that all the congregants minister to one another. But even in these groups, practices counter such claims of equality.

For example, there is almost always a minister, pastor, or rabbi in charge, whose theological and other opinions carry more weight than those of an individual congregant. The worship service is almost always held with the congregants seated and facing the minister or rabbi who is usually elevated above the congregation (in some Anglican and Roman Catholic cathedrals the elevation of the person preaching the sermon is several feet above the heads of the congregants).

Jewish and Christian belief systems reveal what is probably the root of such authoritarian practices: a hierarchy that places divinity (God or the trinity of Father, Son, and Holy Ghost) above men, who are above women, who are above (but not very far above) nature. This gives the one (or the three-in-one) at the top control over those beneath. God is in control of man, man is in control of woman and, as we are told in the Bible, God has given him (in the very first delegation of power) "dominion"—the right to dominate—Earth (nature).

The effect of this model upon religion, upon our social systems, and on our ecological crisis, has been documented.[1]

Contemporary Goddess spirituality groups depart from this model in concept, in the way groups are structured, and in the forms of worship. Hierarchy is a concept foreign to Goddess spirituality. The Goddess and nature are one, and women and men are part of nature and part of the Goddess, as she is part of them.

Worship, usually called ritual or celebration, is almost always conducted in a circle or, if the group is very large, in as close to a circle as can be approximated (e.g., semicircle, ellipse). Leadership is shared, often rotated, among members of a group, and all group members are usually invited to help plan and create a ritual as well as participate in it. There is no sermon, but rather a time for sharing of thoughts during which all who wish to can speak.

This format reflects concepts that are nonauthoritarian. It encourages the development of leadership skills among all members, and it fosters creativity.

The religions that most of us grew up in were based on revelations of prophets and other special "masters." This is the basis of the Bible and of the Qu'ran (also transliterated Koran). Special people had special visions, or special visits from God, making them higher authorities and also in some cases better—more spiritual, closer to God—than the rest of us. In many Eastern religions core beliefs are also determined by masters, gurus, and other authority figures.

Not so in modern Goddess spirituality. All are considered equal in spiritual authority, for Goddess flows though each of us and so none of us is closer to her than another of us. Happily, leaders do arise. Some groups have high priestesses, for example, but they are usually considered teachers—or simply those who have more experience—rather than people who determine which spiritual beliefs or practices are right and which are wrong. And often the role of "high priestess" or other leadership is rotated among members of the group.

IMMANENCE AND TRANSCENDENCE

It has been said that the Goddess is not simply the biblical Father God in a skirt.

What then is she? How is she different from the patriarchal male god? Understanding the difference between the concepts of immanence and transcendence of divinity is crucial to understanding perhaps the most basic difference between Goddess spirituality and patriarchal religions (apart from the obvious difference in gender of divinity).

A transcendent divinity is the concept most of us grew up with. This is the deity, often characterized as God the Father, who exists outside his creation. He created heaven and Earth in six days and on the seventh he rested. He set the planets spinning and the stars shining. He created, molded, a man from a lump of earth and then removed a rib from the man to form a woman. (This is one of the most obvious reversals in the Bible: a man "gives birth" to a woman. An equivalent of this in Greek mythology is Athena springing from the brow of Zeus.) This transcendent God lays down the laws for nature and people to follow. It is even sung of him that "He's got the whole world in his hands."

To contact this deity you must petition, cajole, promise, plead, sacrifice, and bargain. Sometimes you must get another person—a minister, rabbi, priest, a pope, a son, a saint—to intervene for you. And then, if you're lucky, you can get the attention of this Supreme Being—who is out there somewhere running the show.

A transcendent divinity exists apart from creation and the created. I call him God the Manipulator.

Immanent divinity, on the other hand, exists within the created and is the creation. Rather than laying down the law, she is the (natural) law. She is in a continual process of giving birth, dying, and renewal in which the created/creation participates. Rather than holding the world, she is the world.

This concept is organic: all that is exists in an interconnected flow. I call this concept Goddess the Process.

To connect with this divinity you go within, for she flows within you, she flows within all. The path to an immanent divinity therefore is meditation, singing, dancing, art, and simply being "in" nature.

How easy is it to understand and accept a wholly immanent divinity?

In some Pagan groups, there is a tradition in ritual of going around the circle and saying to the person next to you "Thou art Goddess (or God, depending on the person's gender)." Or, as Barbara G. Walker suggests, the ultimate answer to the question "Who is our Goddess?" is "Behold, She is ourselves."[2]

These statements make me and many other people feel uncomfortable; deep within there is something about them that does not entirely ring true. To me, the biggest problem is that they imply that I alone am the deity. I don't think this is the intent of these statements, but I do think this is what a person may come to think upon repeating them. For in religion, especially when statements are ritually repeated, they are often understood and taken literally. I believe what is really meant and what should be clearly stated is that I am part of Goddess and Goddess is part of me; that Goddess flows through me and through all other people. She infuses all nature. We are part of divinity—not apart from divinity. This I believe is the crucial distinction between patriarchal transcendent deities and the contemporary concept of the Goddess.

For some involved in Goddess spirituality, the wholly immanent divinity is most meaningful. For others, divinity is immanent—but also something more. Transcendent is not the right description, for deity does not exist apart from—or above—creation. Rather, both creation and creator blend and flow into one another creating a synergy. This is similar to the concept called "panentheism" in which all of creation exists within or as part of deity or divinity (as distinct from "pantheism" in which divinity infuses matter). Yet this understanding of Goddess as "something more than immanence" goes even beyond panentheism because energy is exchanged between the creator and the created. This synergistic divinity is individual people, animals, Earth, the planets—yet it is also greater than the sum of these parts. It provides guidance, inspiration, and healing that we, as individuals or even as a group, cannot provide on our own.

Goddess is within each of us and we are within her. She flows through all; she flows outwardly to connect us to one another and to nature in which she is also immanent. Yet she is certainly more than any single individual, and may in a sense be greater than all of creation, while still containing—or being one with—the creation rather than being apart from it.

This paradox is the core of her mystery.

NATURE OF THE GODDESS

Other questions about the nature of the Goddess also continue to be topics of discussion and wondering: Is the Goddess one or many? Is she a Being (or many beings)? A form of energy? A metaphor?

Before patriarchy, in the beginning the Goddess was One. I think it is fair to say at that time, she was viewed as a Being. In some cultures, such as those in Africa, she was indistinguishable from—or grew out of—belief in a common ancestress.

As peoples migrated they took their concept of Goddess with them. But as they continued living apart from their original group, the concept underwent changes. For a while, in some cultures she remained one Goddess with names varying according to language and culture. Later she became a multiplicity of goddesses, each with different functions or characteristics. This fragmentation appears to parallel the rise of patriarchy. In some cultures she was both one and three: the triune Goddess—Maiden or Virgin (corresponding to the new moon/waxing crescent), Mother (corresponding to the full moon), and Crone (corresponding the waning crescent). She often had a son/consort, the God. Representing the cycles of the seasons, he died at harvest and was born again at the winter solstice. Eventually, as patriarchy progressed, the son/consort gods became more powerful than the goddesses. For example, in the Greek and Roman pantheons the goddesses were demoted to being the wives and daughters of the much more powerful gods.

With this history, what is the belief about the Goddess or goddesses today? The answer varies greatly from individual to individual—and that's okay!

Some view the Goddess as One. Some view her as one with three aspects. Others view her as one with many aspects. And still others feel more comfortable with a multiplicity of separate goddesses (and sometimes gods) often to reflect what they feel to be their own many aspects and potentialities.

Today those who consider the Goddess (and God) or goddesses (and gods) discrete beings are not in the majority. Far more common is a concept, similar to that proposed by Mary Daly, which says that divinity, rather than being a noun—or a Being—is a verb: Be-ing.[3] Others consider Goddess a term for a form of energy or a metaphor.

What does it mean to say Goddess is a form of energy?

In her 1935 book, *The Mystical Qabalah*, Dion Fortune discusses the question of whether deities are "real"—that is, exist apart from human invention—or whether they are entirely created by people. Her answer is somewhere in between—or rather, a combination. Spiritual—or what Fortune calls "as-

tral"—forms, are real, but without what we would call personality until humans create images to which these forms may attach themselves. A deity is therefore a form of spiritual energy
which has attached itself to a human concept. When this at-
tachment occurs, the concept is no longer imaginary, but becomes real and has power. Further, Fortune says, as long as
people keep the astral form alive by worshipping it, the deity is
"available for contacting, brought down within the range of
human perception. Should the worship cease, the [deity] with-
draws. . . . Should other worshippers come along. . .it is a
comparatively simple matter to attract into the form once more
that life that was accustomed to ensoul it. . . ."[4]

This seems to explain the experience that many people
have of Goddess as a very real source of energy. People beginning anew to worship the Goddess (or individual goddesses)
in a very real sense bring her (or them) back to life. This could
explain the widespread "visions" of goddesses (sometimes identified as the Virgin Mary, especially by Catholics) that have occurred through the centuries and seem to have increased in
the past twenty years.

This co-created divinity is somewhere between concrete
personification of deity as a discrete being and deity as purely
spiritual energy. Understanding Goddess as spiritual energy
means that we accept that there is a spiritual dimension to the
universe, that we can (and do) interact with this dimension,
and that this dimension is best understood when characterized as Goddess. We can give Goddess personal characteristics
and names, such as Astarte, Kwan Yin, Kali, Venus, Oya, Diana,
Isis, etc., or we can simply call the spiritual energy Goddess, or
Great Mother and describe her with feminine imagery. This is
distinct from—but close to—understanding Goddess as metaphor.

The difference between understanding Goddess as energy
and Goddess as metaphor is that to understand the former,

you need to accept that there is a spiritual dimension to the universe. If you cannot accept this (and there are some individuals involved in Goddess spirituality who are not comfortable with that concept—who believe that the world, the universe, consists of matter only and when you die there is no separate spiritual part of you that survives), then you can still understand and honor the Goddess as a metaphor for the natural world, which is divine. The question then becomes, if Goddess is simply a metaphor, why call it Goddess? Why not God? Or, for that matter, Dog?

My answer is: Because metaphors matter. The metaphor we use for divinity matters because it affects and is reflected in almost every other facet of society. The metaphor we use for divinity matters in our initial access to divinity, in our ultimate understanding of divinity, and in the resulting community.

For example, if our metaphor for divinity is God the Manipulator who exists outside creation, who molds and forms the universe and all that is within (including us), and who lays down the law, our initial access to divinity is daunting, achievable mainly through cajoling and bargaining—and we may need an intermediary. Our ultimate understanding of this deity is that he is a manipulative creator of a mechanistic universe in which the role of man (sic) is to subdue nature. Resulting communities are likely to be hierarchical, competitive, and violent.[5]

If our metaphor for divinity is Goddess the Process who is one with the universe, who is natural "law," our initial access to this immanent and synergistic divinity is immediate and easy through inner focus and group ritual. Our ultimate understanding of divinity is that she is one with her creation, that the creator and created are in constant flow, that the universe is interactive and in constant flux; and that we are to live as part of nature. Resulting communities are likely to be egalitarian, cooperative, and peaceful. [6]

DUALITIES

Goddess spirituality resists opposing dualities and dichotomies. For example, female and male are seen not as opposites
but as complementary. Similarly "light" and "dark" are not
considered to represent the oppositional forces of "good" and
"evil" as is often the case in Jewish and Christian symbolism.
Rather, light and dark are each seen as essential to one another, and each is understood as playing an essential role in
spirituality.

Darkness is conceived as womblike, as representing our
inner selves and the ability to go deeply within. Darkness is
the source of creative activity, including spiritual work. It also
represents death, which is understood as a transformative phase
of the cycle of nature leading to rebirth. Light is the product
of creative activity, the concrete manifestation of spirit. Light
is what we are born into, it is also that which is born.

Despite this emphasis on complementariness and completeness, there are a few concepts in Goddess spirituality that
may seem to depend on dichotomies. For example, assigning
feminine gender to the Moon (as in Mother Moon, and the
triple Goddess's relation to Moon phases) appears to give cre-
dence to the dichotomies of female=passive versus male=active
if viewed through the concept that the Moon merely reflects
energy and is therefore passive in relation to the Sun. In this
duality, the Sun would be seen as male and active (this concept
is apparent in traditional astrology interpretations, for instance).

However, let's consider the Moon as a symbol of the divine female from two other points of view. First, in prehistory
where this concept originated, it was not known that the Moon's
light was a reflection of the Sun. Rather, the Moon was seen as
beautiful, mysterious but predictable in its changeability, and
powerful—night's brightest light. The similarity of the Moon's
cycle to the approximately twenty-eight days of a woman's men-

strual cycle seemed to indicate an affinity between the Moon and women. (It should be noted, however, that some ancient cultures had moon gods and sun goddesses.) Second, from a contemporary scientific point of view, we know that the Moon is not passive, but plays an active role in sustaining life as we know it on Earth through regulation of the tides and other gravitational functions. Both Sun and Moon are essential to Earth. This reveals the oppositional duality (Sun=male=active versus Moon=female=passive), in which the Moon is equated with the female because of its supposed passivity, to be an erroneous construct rationalized from faulty science.

The personifications "Mother Earth" and "Father Sky" express another apparent duality. Such characterization is often used in ecologically involved groups as a way of including all of nature in divinity while honoring both the female and male.

I think this dichotomy bears examination. The "sky" is part of Earth, since it is the planet's atmosphere. Is this what is meant by "Father Sky?" Or is "sky" being used as a place separate from Earth, perhaps as a synonym for "heaven" or some other transcendent location? If so, this presents us with the old hierarchical and stereotypical duality of female=Earth=instinct versus male=sky=intellect. If this is not what we mean, we should be clear on exactly what our meaning is. Otherwise, because of our cultural conditioning, the message our subconscious gets when we call Earth "Mother" while calling the sky "Father" is that intellect is a male quality while females operate on an instinctual level. I don't think this is the message we want to give ourselves and our children. Therefore, I would call for a close examination of these and other dualities that involve male versus female roles and qualities before we use them in our ritual work.

This discussion brings us to a question that often arises in feminist/women's/Goddess spirituality: How do we (or do we?) incorporate male as divine? This is a problem because of the persisting image of the patriarchal god. He is, to many, a male run amok. Originally the son/consort of the Goddess but transformed by patriarchy into a selfish dictator, he banished and vilified the Goddess and degraded women. If we allow a male image into Goddess spirituality, some ask, will he get out of control and take over again?

In reaction, some groups that embrace Goddess spirituality do not include any male deity or male imaging of the divine. Goddess, they say, includes all and is all you need, whether you are male or female. Others, following a more traditional Pagan path, honor both the Goddess and the God as her son/consort. He is seen as her helper and companion, and instrumental to Earth's natural cycles.

My solution to this quandary has been to image divinity as Great Mother who dwells with the Father, her Son. They are One in what I chose to call the Eternal Spirit, which I image as Light.

This I conceived in the late 1970s, when first exploring Goddess spirituality. It has been confirmed by my later explorations of Kabbalah.

GUIDED MEDITATIONS

TRANSITION FROM TRANSCENDENT TO IMMANENT DIVINITY

Sit in a comfortable position with both feet on the floor and your hands unclasped. Take several deep breaths and let these breaths bring relaxation into your body.

(Pause)

And as you continue breathing deeply, let your mind go back in time, back to the time when you were a child. And now you are a child sitting, looking up into one of your parent's eyes or the eyes of another grownup you love and trust. You listen as this person tells you a story about an Old Man With A

White Beard way up above you, high up in the sky. With your child's eye you can see this man, whom your parent calls the Heavenly Father, you can see him floating way above you in the sky. You reach up for him, but he floats up out of reach—higher and higher he soars, until he is outside Earth's atmosphere. As he goes higher, he gets bigger, so you can still see him as he soars outside our solar system, getting bigger and bigger he moves outside our universe as you watch from way down below, so far away.

The story ends, and looking into your parent's eyes, you see your wonder reflected there.

(Pause)

Now see yourself as seven or eight years old. You still think about this story, sometimes you may even pray to the Heavenly Father, whom you have been taught to also call God. But you have a hard time remembering what he looks like. (Pause)

You grow older, now you are ten or eleven, and as is common with children that age, you have a problem: perhaps it is at school or with a friend or a teacher or one of your parents. Remember such a problem in your past. (Pause) You need help, so again you try to pray to the Heavenly Father, you pour out your heart to him. (Pause)

But nothing happens. (Pause)

You try again. You picture the Old Man With A White Beard up in heaven and you beg and plead, promising to do whatever he wants in return for help. As you finish, you notice a string up in the sky. With your inner eye, follow the string upward and see that it leads to the large, powerful hands of the Heavenly Father. From his hands you watch the string come down, down, down until it is connected to the top of your head.

You move your head, thinking you will get his attention when he feels the string in his hand move, but he doesn't respond. You look up and see many other strings that go from his hands to everybody else on Earth—as well as to the Moon, stars, and all the planets. You watch as he pulls the strings at his will and the object attached to that string responds. He draws one of them, connected to our globe, Earth, up, up, up into his hands. He's got the whole world in his hands and when you realize this, you remember singing a song about it. (Pause)

As you grow older, you push this experience—along with other childhood memories—to the back of your mind. Time goes by. You finish school, perhaps you fall in love, launch a career, and are at a crucial time of transition in your life.

Remember how this time felt, or feels—for you may be in such a time in your life now. (Pause)

You have almost forgotten about the string that attaches you to the Heavenly Father when you feel a yank on your head. And you also feel tugs on your hands and you see strings are also attached to your hands. They go up, up, up to the Old Man With A White Beard.

Why is he pulling the strings? What is it he wants you to do? (Pause)

You do what you think he wants now. (Pause)

How does it make you feel? (Pause)

Although you may have accepted the experience at first, as it continues, it becomes uncomfortable for you: you feel diminished—like a servant. Yet you are afraid to detach yourself from him because of your belief—shared by everyone you know—in his power over you, over the world, over the universe. (Pause)

But even as your discomfort increases, you feel yourself growing stronger and more sure of yourself. You begin to feel confident in relying on your own experiences, your own knowledge that dwells deep within you. And you come to understand that the strings are there only because you accept them, and that the Old Man is only as real as you allow him to be. So, eyeing those strings once more, you take a deep breath and look around for something to cut them with.

(Pause)

Now you see what you will use.

(Pause)

Take it and, when you are ready, sever this oppressive tie.

(Pause)

You cut the strings and immediately you are set free and you float, you float into light-filled space. How does it feel? Scary? Exhilarating?

As you float you see others who have similarly freed themselves and you float together in the light. And as you recognize each other, fine filaments of light flow from each person. They solidify, intertwine, connecting you to one another yet allowing for personal freedom. You move, and through the connection the others gently move too: they move as you move—gently, gently, you move into a dance, a dance that weaves you all together. And together you float down to Earth and, in a circle with the others now, you send a filament down to the center of the earth and breathe in deeply, bringing Earth's energy up into you.

Experience this energy as it fills you. How does it feel?

(Pause)

Now you all extend your filaments, your threads, upwards to the skies—to the Sun and the Moon and all the planets of the solar system—and receive, as you take a deep breath, the energy of light.

Experience this energy as it fills you. How does this energy differ from Earth's energy?

(Pause)

Now you and the others send your threads out even further into the universe and receive the energy of the Vast Womb, the energy of the Mother of all. She who encompasses all, yet who dwells in each. She who connects all. She who is the filaments through whom we receive the power of Earth, the power of light, and the life of her womb. She who connects all. She who flows through all.

And now through these filaments of light, send out what good you will: to each other, and in thanksgiving down into the earth, and up to the skies, and out into the universe that is her womb.

For this connection works both ways—works all ways. For in the Goddess we are connected to one another, to Earth and to the universe. She in us. We in her.

Now take several deep breaths.

Become aware once again of your body, and remember your surroundings. Then when you are ready, slowly open your eyes and come back to this time and this place.

NEW MOON: A MEDITATION ON DARKNESS AND LIGHT

Sit in a comfortable position with both feet on the ground, hands in a relaxed position on your lap or beside your body. Take several deep breaths, and as you breathe slowly in and out, feel an increasing sense of relaxation.

(Pause)

In your mind's eye you see that darkness surrounds you. Below, the ground is dark—the darkness of Earth. Above, the sky is dark—the inky darkness of night with no moon and no stars visible. And all around you is dark. Do you feel comfortable in this darkness? If you do, continue to rest, relax, float in the darkness.

If you feel any fear in this darkness, focus on it now. What is it you're afraid of?

(Pause)

This fear may come from what your culture has taught you about darkness. Or it may come from a real and scary experience you had in the dark.

Whatever the source, focus on it now. What does it look like? (Pause)

As you see your fear now, you can make it smaller. Make it smaller and smaller until you can take it in your hand. Take it in your hand now and as you do, understand that it cannot harm you. Close your hand around it and make a tight fist. (Pause) Open your fist now. Is there anything there? (Pause) If not, know that you have overcome your fear. If there is still something in your hand, however small, let go of it. Push it away. Propel it into the darkness and know that it goes now to a place where it can harm no one, including you.

(Pause)

Become conscious of the darkness once again, the dark of Earth below you, of the inky sky above you, of the night that surrounds you. Feel now how your senses become more acute in the dark. You can hear better. Your eyes adjust so you can see better, and you can sense what you could not when it was light. And now breathe in from the darkness below you that is Earth, the nourishment—the potential for growth—that Earth offers you.

(Pause)

Now become conscious of the darkness that surrounds you, feel it as the arms of a Great Mother in whose embrace you nestle though the night: safe, safe, safe as can be.

(Pause)

Now focus on the darkness above you, the darkness of the night's sky. Let your eyes scan the sky, first directly above you, and then down, down towards the horizon. (Pause)

And as you look, slowly, slowly, the dark brings forth a silver sliver of light just above the horizon. And you look upon the first light of the new moon.

Welcome the new moon now, in your own way.

(Pause)

And now, as the moon becomes brighter, sense the strength that it brings: the strength of growth, for this silver sliver will soon grow into the Mighty Maiden of the waxing crescent—independent and whole unto herself. As she brings light to the darkness, she brings the courage to start anew. Now she offers to share her strength and courage with you for whatever you need it for in the month ahead. If you wish, accept, take in, this strength and courage in a way that is comfortable for you.

(Pause)

Now once again shift your gaze in the night sky and notice how the stars are beginning to become visible. And as you watch the stars come out, one light in particular catches your eye. Perhaps it's a star, or maybe it's something else, but its shimmer seems to be calling to you. (Pause)

This light now starts to take another shape, the shape of something to come for you this month—a project, a plan, a hope, a relationship, an activity—something you will begin this month. Watch as this light emerges from the darkness into the shape of your new beginning.

(Pause)

And now, if you wish, in a way that is comfortable for you, take this light with its own special shape inside you, so that it becomes part of you, so that its light becomes your light.

(Pause)

And now trust that as you have shaped this light from darkness, so you can shape your success for the coming month.

(Pause)

And now, in your own way, give thanks for the help you receive now and will receive this month in all you achieve.

(Pause)

And when you are ready, slowly and comfortably, come back to this time and place.

New Moon Ritual

In ancient times, the new moon was celebrated when the first sliver of the waxing moon could be seen above the horizon. Today new moon celebrations are often held on any of the nights from the new to the waxing crescent phases.

If you or your group are new to Goddess spirituality, and you want to get a feeling for the difference between the usual patriarchal authoritarian format of having one (often elevated) leader facing the congregation and the matrifocal format of a circle with shared leadership, you may want to do this ritual first in the authoritarian format with one person leading on an elevated platform and the rest of the people sitting, facing the leader. The altar should also be on the platform. Then do the ritual a second time with everyone seated in a circle with the role of leader rotated among as many people as possible. The altar should be placed in the center of the circle. The group can then discuss the differences in how each of these formats felt to the participants and to the leader(s).

If you've been involved in Goddess spirituality for some time, you may want to do only the shared leadership format, or simply incorporate some or all of the material in this ritual into your own practice.

The instructions for the shared leadership format are italicized. Instructions for the authoritarian format are in roman type. Those that apply to both formats are also in italics. Spoken words are boldfaced.

On the altar are symbols of the four directions and elements and a freshly baked loaf of bread (in crescent shape, if possible) or freshly baked croissants. Representations of the Maiden aspect of the Goddess may also be placed on the altar.

Purification

To distance ourselves from the past month's problems, we "purify" with salt water, which is known to have healing powers. Quiet music is helpful during this part of the ritual.

In the authoritarian format, each person comes to the platform and the leader places a drop of salt water on each person's forehead.

In the shared leadership format, the bowl of salt water is passed to the left around the circle. The person on the right, holds the bowl for the person on her left, who places drops of water on herself where she feels the need for healing.

Calling of Directions

In the authoritarian format, one person reads the whole "calling of directions."

In a shared leadership circle format, the calling can be done in any of several ways:

* each direction can be spoken by a different person

* each direction can be spoken by all people standing when the direction is spoken

* everyone can say the first and last lines for each direction, while a different individual —or all persons located at that direction—speak the second through fifth lines.

In groups that cast a circle, the calling of directions may follow the custom of the group. In many groups, this involves one person going around the outside of the circle, defining sacred space, as the directions are called. An alternative is to wait until the directions have all been called and then have everyone join hands, close their eyes and visualize light encircling all present.

We honor the East
Home of air
March wind
Morning's song
Eagle's flight
Aurora's breath
Welcome East

We honor the South
Home of fire
Noon sun
Flame of change
Heat of passion
Pele's power
Welcome South

We honor the West
Home of water
River's flow
Font of feelings
World's womb
Kwan Yin's love
Welcome West

We honor the North
Home of Earth
Root of life
Shaded mystery
Ground of being
Gaia's growth
Welcome North.

New Moon Invocation

In the authoritarian format, the invocation is spoken by the leader.

In the shared leadership format, the invocation may be spoken by one person or by everyone together.

> **Mighty Maiden**
> **Month's first light**
> **Send us your strength**
> **this holy night.**
> **Shine your blessings**
> **on us all**
> **so that with you**
> **we may grow whole:**
> **True to ourselves**
> **in all we begin,**
> **True to our vision**
> **in all we attain.**

Guided Meditation

In both formats, the leader guides the group in a meditation: the meditations provided in this chapter, or any other appropriate meditation, may be used.

Plans for the Month

In the authoritarian format, the leader, standing on the platform in front of the group, gives a lecture/sermon of about ten minutes on the subject of making new plans or goals for the coming month.

In the shared leadership format, all participants in the circle are given a chance to speak about their plans and goals for the coming month. If the new moon meditation provided in this chapter is used, participants may want to share what shape the light in the meditation took for them. Each person may place on the altar a symbol of a new project, plan, hope, etc. Alternately, participants may light candles representing their plans.

Chant

In the authoritarian format, the leader specifies words or sounds having to do with new plans for the group to chant. For example, "work," "love," "success." The leader starts and guides the chant, with all participants singing the same words and melody at the same time.

In the shared leadership format the chant is either allowed to arise spontaneously or a person other than the leader is chosen to start it with a single word or sound. No specific words or sounds are suggested. The only instructions are that group members will chant their projects, hopes, goals, and plans into being.

For example, a person hoping to initiate a love relationship can sing the word "love" or the name of the beloved. A person planning to start a new job can chant "new job" or be more specific and sing the name of the company it's with. Or, people can simply chant vowels or other sounds that to them correspond to their goal, project, hope, or plan. It is not expected that everyone will be chanting the same word or sound. In fact, the very difference in—and interweaving of—words, sounds, and melodies are what make this way of chanting exciting.

Nourishment

In the authoritarian format, the leader distributes bread or croissants to each person saying, **"Be nourished, that her strength and courage may become yours."**

In the shared leadership format, the plate of bread or croissants is passed around the circle. As each person passes the bread to the person on the right, she says the same phrase as above.

Releasing Directions

In the authoritarian format, the leader speaks the "calling" in reverse order (starting with North), substituting **"Farewell"** for "Welcome."

In the shared leadership format, the same may be done, but with four different leaders speaking or all participants taking part, as in the "calling." Or the first and last lines may be spoken by all, but in between individuals extemporaneously offer their words to release and thank the elements and directions. This can bring to the "releasing" meaning that is more personal and perhaps more relevant to what has transpired.

Blessing

In the authoritarian format, the leader speaks this blessing.

In the shared leadership format, all stand and hold hands while speaking this together or echoing it back to a leader.

**Valiant Virgin we thank you
for being with us tonight.
Your strength and courage infuse us
with the blessing of growing light.**

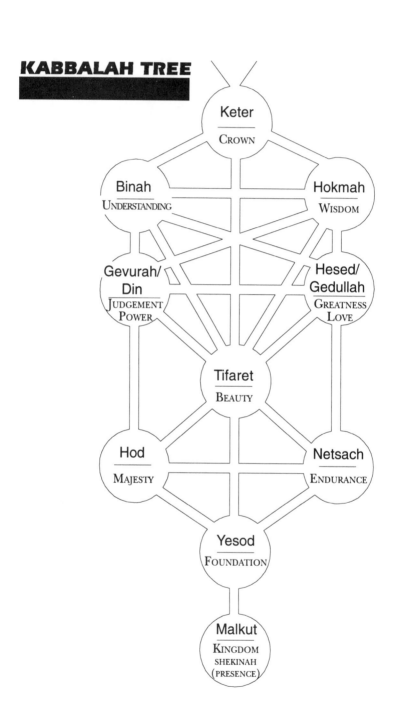

KABBALAH TREE

Keter
CROWN

Binah
UNDERSTANDING

Hokmah
WISDOM

Gevurah/
Din
JUDGEMENT
POWER

Hesed/
Gedullah
GREATNESS
LOVE

Tifaret
BEAUTY

Hod
MAJESTY

Netsach
ENDURANCE

Yesod
FOUNDATION

Malkut
KINGDOM
SHEKINAH
(PRESENCE)

Chapter 2
Kabbalah: In Its Beginnings

Say to Wisdom: "You are my sister."
Join thought to divine wisdom, so she and he become one.
—Proverbs 7:4 as elaborated by Azriel of Gerona, thirteenth-century kabbalist

↜ LIKE TODAY'S OTHER mainstream religions most of Judaism's religious practices are patriarchal. Yet in its traditions are also found remnants of the Middle Eastern Goddess religions which preceded it. In fact, contrary to widespread assumptions, there is considerable evidence that only in recent years has Judaism become a totally monotheistic male-god-only religion.[1]

Some of the more widely known examples of the persistence of prepatriarchal practices are the definition of a Jew by matrilineal descent, long a de facto practice and since the establishment of the state of Israel, a legal fact; the custom of a woman lighting the Sabbath candles to "bring in" the Sabbath, a tradition probably related to her being identified with the Shekinah, God's feminine aspect, also called the "Sabbath Queen"; and the use of lunar months in the Hebrew calendar.

As we shall discover, Kabbalah, though greatly transformed by patriarchy, also derives from earlier matrifocal religious practices. And we shall also see that the "secret" it has been carrying according to tradition—the great mystery nestled in the branches of "the Tree"—is the knowledge of the Goddess, not merely as the feminine aspect of God identified with the bottom of the Tree, but as the totality of creation.

To understand how this came to be, we will look first at traditional Jewish Kabbalah's myriad beliefs. We will then move on to how mostly non-Jewish mystics of the Western esoteric tradition, transliterating the word "Qabalah," adapted it to incorporate additional metaphysical beliefs.

Transliterated from Hebrew, Kabbalah (or Qabalah) means "that which is received from ancient times." It is represented by a glyph called "the Tree of Life" or often simply "the Tree." Because many words used to describe and talk about Kabbalah are transliterated from Hebrew, their spellings vary from source to source. On the Tree are round objects, called by their Hebrew name, "sefirot" (singular, "sefirah"). The sefirot are connected by branches called "channels" or "paths." There are ten sefirot. Their most commonly accepted names and meanings in Jewish Kabbalah are shown in the accompanying drawing.

Jewish Kabbalah is not one set of beliefs, but rather a variety of beliefs and practices drawn from a number of sources, which changed, evolved—some might say mutated—over the centuries.

Traditionally in Judaism restrictions were placed on who could study Kabbalah. Usually you had to be at least forty years old and married. (However, two of the greatest kabbalists, Moses Cordovero and Isaac Luria, began their studies well before this age.) You had to have high moral standards, prior religious studies, and be emotionally stable. And you had to be a man. A concept central to Jewish Kabbalah is that the separation of Shekinah (the feminine divine) from God occurred in the Garden of Eden when Adam mistook the lowest sefirah, Malkut (synonymous with Shekinah), for the entirety of divinity. This mistake caused Shekinah to be separated from God. The goal of much of the prayer and meditation of

Kabbalah (especially, as we shall see, of Lurianic Kabbalah) is the reuniting of the Shekinah with the male God. Kabbalists believe this reunion will enable the arrival of the Messiah.

The implications of this myth for feminist/women's/Goddess spirituality are vast. In this myth, Adam's sin is related to Goddess worship and reinforces the more obvious symbols of Goddess condemnation in Genesis such as the vilification of the serpent—long a symbol of healing and regeneration and of the Goddess—the fruit from the Tree of Knowledge (the "apple" or pomegranate" are also symbols of the Goddess) and the Tree itself, which probably originally represented the Hebrew/Canaanite Goddess Asherah (whose symbol was a tree). These and other ramifications of kabbalistic thought are almost always disregarded or overlooked.

To better understand these ideas, and to get to the Goddess root, we need to start at the beginning—or as near the beginning as we can get—and see how belief upon belief, myth upon myth, were heaped on the branches of the Tree until finally her original shape became entirely obscured.

Though Kabbalah in Judaism didn't emerge as a strong literary form until the thirteenth century and attained its greatest popularity in the sixteenth and seventeenth centuries, according to tradition, Kabbalah existed from the beginning of human life.

WHAT THE BIBLE TELLS US

According to tradition, Kabbalah was given to Adam in the Garden of Eden. At first these teachings were secret, and their transmission oral. Also according to tradition, the first written description of Kabbalah is credited to the first biblical patriarch, Abraham.

Kabbalists reading the Bible see evidence of kabbalistic thought throughout. There is even a tradition which asserts that the written Torah (first five books of the Hebrew Scripture) is only a surface Torah; that the real Torah can only be perceived by "reading between the lines." The written Torah is traditionally attributed to the sefirah, Tifaret, while the oral Torah is identified with Malkut (Shekinah), one of whose epithet's is "the mouth."[2]

However, this dual attribution is probably one of the many attempts we will find as we explore Kabbalah to lessen the importance of the female divine. In the early twelfth century, kabbalists considered Shekinah synonymous with Torah, regardless of whether Torah was oral or written. It wasn't until the thirteenth century that the distinction of oral as feminine and written as masculine began to be made. In kabbalists' view, the Torah scroll then became a phallic symbol, with the crown atop it being its feminine part.[3]

Certain biblical passages become very important in kabbalistic thought. These include the creation story, Isaiah's vision of God enthroned in the Temple accompanied by angels, and the opening of the book of Ezekiel (which is dated about 6 B.C.E.). The latter includes the vision of the chariot, in which the prophet sees a throne containing a humanlike figure surrounded by a rainbowlike radiance, spinning through heaven accompanied by four winged creatures.[4] These creatures or cherubim, which always appear in pairs, are sometimes represented as male and female, sometimes both female.[5]

This vision of the chariot became the central image of merkavah (chariot) mysticism, a form of kabbalistic thought in which the worshipper made his body the "divine chariot" or vehicle to attract the Shekinah. That is, the worshipper became a "vessel" or "chariot" for her.

In the *Sefir Yetsirah* (Book of Creation), the first kabbalistic writings, attributed to Abraham but thought to be written 200-500 C.E., the creation is said to have been an act of divine speech, as in Gen. 1:3: "And God *said*, Let there be light and there was light," (emphasis mine).

Another important biblical concept with kabbalistic ramifications is that of the Hebrew term "Hokmah," meaning Wisdom (in Greek, Sophia). Throughout the Bible, Hokmah is spoken of in female terms. For example in Proverbs 8: "Doth not wisdom cry? And understanding put forth her voice? She standeth in the top of high places, by the way, where paths meet, she standeth. . . ." Here wisdom and understanding (later commonly understood as separate sefirot) appear to either be synonymous or both female. In addition, "she standeth in the top of high places" can be understood as a reference to the Hebrew/Canaanite Goddess Asherah, whose altars were built atop hills and other high places. Wisdom continues to speak: "The Lord possessed me in the beginning of his way, before the works of old. I was set up from everlasting, from the beginning, or ever the earth was. . . . Then I was by him, as one brought up with him. . . . Blessed is the man that heareth me. . . . For whoso findeth me findeth life, and shall obtain favour of the Lord. But he that sinneth against me wrongeth his own soul: all that hate me love death."

Clearly this biblical passage rings with the voice of female divinity, called Wisdom.

Similarly, in Proverbs 9, we read: "Wisdom hath builded her house, she hath hewn out her seven pillars. . .as for him that wanteth understanding, she saith to him: Come, eat of my bread, and drink of the wine which I have mingled. . . ."

In addition, in early Jewish mysticism, Wisdom was synonymous with Torah, the "word of God."[6]

In Kabbalah, however, Hokmah becomes male, the "supernal father" and is the first emanation from the Keter or "nothingness."

What does all this mean in terms of the origins of Kabbalah?

First, it is clear that according to tradition, Kabbalah has existed as long as humans have—that is, it existed in some form from prehistoric times.

Second, it has undergone enormous changes, first in its oral tradition, and then in its written explanations.

And third, and most tantalizing, these changes have included reversals of the original intent, one instance of which is the gender reversal of Hokmah (Wisdom), a female noun in Hebrew which is consistently personified as female in Scripture and other writings. This reversal of Hokmah, together with the shift in symbolism of Torah from wholly female to mostly male, is our first inkling of more extensive reversals and changes.

Sefir Yetsirah and Other Early Influences

In the third to sixth centuries C.E., merkavah mysticism developed to include magical teachings. The teachings linked to Ezekiel's vision of the chariot were similar to Greek and Gnostic Sophia teachings.[7] Observances included the singing of "chariot" hymns which always included the refrain "Holy, Holy, Holy is the Lord of Hosts. The whole earth is filled with his presence or (sometimes translated glory)." This passage is still used as the sanctification in both the Jewish and Christian religions.

The use of the words "glory" and "presence" is interesting, as glory (koved, in Hebrew), is a masculine noun which came to have two meanings during this time. It meant both the name of God when used in mystical inquiry, and was a name given to an area of theosophical research. The term "presence," meaning the Shekinah, came to be associated with the feminine manifestation of God that dwelled in the chariot. The goal of the participant in merkavah mysticism was to ascend to the throne and thus to "glory," which is envisioned as a "supernal man" sitting on the throne.[8]

Jewish gnosticism, another mystical movement at this time, was mostly concerned with the creation (in Hebrew ma'aseh bereshit) and with the ten "sayings by which the world was created." These sayings became ten divine qualities. This thread of mysticism may have also included speculation about what is called in Kabbalah the "Adam Kadmon," as described in Genesis 1:26: "And God said, Let us make man in our image. . . ."[9] (The use of the pronoun "us" here stems from the use of the Hebrew noun "Elohim" in the original, which is usually translated "God" with a solely male connotation, but which is a plural noun encompassing both female and male.)

The *Sefir Yetsirah*, purporting to reveal the secrets of creation, contains the first written mention of the "thirty-two wondrous paths" consisting of ten sefirot, which it describes as "entities of emptiness," and twenty-two elemental letters. A further description indirectly shows a link with Goddess beliefs: "Their measure is ten, yet infinite. Their end is embedded in their beginning, their beginning in their end. . ." This description is that of the uroboros, a depiction of the universe as a snake swallowing its tail, an ancient Goddess symbol and credited here to the influence of the Ophitic (Jewish snake worshipping) sect.[10]

Consisting of fewer than 2,000 words, *Sefir Yetsirah* nevertheless extensively influenced later kabbalistic thought. It includes, according to Gershom Scholem, the "Judaizing" of non-Jewish concepts. For example, the idea of Shekinah in part originated with the Gnostic idea of a divine spark in exile on Earth. Later, this combined with Jewish ideas, including that of a heavenly entity called "Shekinah" representing the earthly community of Israel (in Hebrew, knesset Israel). The feminine noun "Shekinah" comes from the biblical Hebrew verb "shakkan" (to dwell), and its first meaning was that aspect of deity that can be apprehended by the senses.[11]

Sefir Yetsirah also contains Jewish thought on divine Wisdom (Hokmah), including the "thirty-two secret paths of divine wisdom." The meaning of sefirot in this work was "numbers" with a mystical allusion to their use in creation. In Hebrew, letters and numbers are represented by the same symbols.

The first sefirah, later called by the masculine noun "Keter" (Crown), was, in this early work called "Ru'ah" (spirit), a feminine noun. In thought that appears to be borrowed from the Greeks, Ru'ah (spirit) emanates the element air as represented in the second sefirah and from air issues the third sefirah, related to the element water, and the fourth sefirah, related to the element fire. The last six sefirot represent the six dimensions of space. Nevertheless, the ten sefirot are a closed unit, as in the outerboros image.

All real beings, the text says, came into existence through the interconnection of the twenty-two Hebrew letters. The first three letters are also related to the seasons, links borrowed by Greek/Hellenistic thought. The first three letters are also related to the head, torso, and stomach. The next seven letters, which are known as double letters in Hebrew, represent the seven planets (known at that time), the seven heavens, seven days of the week, and seven human orifices of the eyes, ears, nostrils, and mouth. The final twelve letters represent the twelve signs of the zodiac, twelve months, and the limbs of the body. This material later evolved into the magical instructions for making a "golem" (synthetic man) and other magical kabbalistic practices.[12]

This demonstrates the importance and specificity of language in kabbalistic thought, and gives us another Goddess

link: the role of language in creation; that of equating creation
with "the word," originally a Goddess epithet.[13]
And we see that not only did the second sefirah, Hokmah,
undergo a sex change, but also the first sefirah, later known by
the male noun "Keter" (Crown) was originally known by the
female noun "Ru'ah" (spirit), a meaning far closer than "crown"
to the "spirit" of the first sefirah—which, we are told, is without gender and is pure spirit beyond human understanding.

MEDIEVAL MYTHOLOGY

Several centuries passed before Kabbalah emerged near
the end of the twelfth century in the Jewish community of
Provence, France, with the circulation of *Sefir ha-Bahir* ("Bright
Book"), the first text to use what has become a typical kabbalistic
approach and symbolic structure. The text states that the term
"sefirah" is not connected with the Greek word meaning sphere,
but rather with the Hebrew word for sapphire. It discusses the
ten sefirot, which it calls (in an elaboration of *Sefir Yetsirah*),
the "ten divine sayings" by which the world was created.[14]

The *Bahir's* main importance in the development of
kabbalistic thought is its use of symbolic language. It inter-
prets Scripture not in terms of worldly events but in terms of
events in the divine world. The sefirot become divine attributes,
rather than numbers, and are variously referred to as beautiful
vessels, kings, voices, and crowns. Introducing the theory of
"transmigration of souls" (reincarnation) into Jewish thought,
this text says that the divine attributes or powers constitute the
"secret tree" from which souls come. We can understand this
as the written incorporation (or emergence) of another Goddess symbol, the Tree, and the implication of the Goddess as
the spiritual source.

From France, kabbalistic thought traveled to Spain, emerging in Toledo at the beginning of the thirteenth century. An

early Spanish kabbalist, Abraham Abulafia of Toledo, advised his fellow kabbalists that the purpose of wearing tallis (prayer shawls) and tefillin (phylacteries, thin leather straps wound around the hands and head, with a stamp-size square worn at the middle of the forehead) was "so that you will be filled with the awe of Shekinah. . . ." To help this process, Abulafia instructed them to visualize the name of God (YHVH) and enter a deep meditative state. Also at this time, elements of Neoplatonic mysticism and speculations about the origins of evil were incorporated into kabbalistic inquiry.[15]

The most important text in Kabbalah according to many kabbalists, the *Sefir-ha Zohar* (Book of Radiance), was written in Aramaic between 1280 and 1286 by Moses de León, a Jew living near Madrid. León is thought to have written at least parts of it in a trance state, that is as "automatic writing."[16]

It is here that we read a description of the Tree as representing the Adam Kadmon (primordial man):

"These bodies are named according to this arrangement: Hesed, the right arm; Gevurah, the left arm; Tif'eret, the trunk of the body; Netsach and Hod, the two legs; Yesod, completion of the body and sign of the holy covenant [the phallus and site of circumcision]; Malkut, the mouth—we call her the oral Torah. Hokhmah is the brain. . .Binah is the heart-mind. . . . Keter elyon is the royal crown, the skull. . . ."[17]

Thus we see the Tree, a symbol of the Goddess, transformed into a man.

In one form of kabbalistic meditation, the meditator imagined himself traveling within the beard of the Adam Kadmon. Since the power to direct the future resided in the oil of the beard, such a meditation gave the kabbalist the ability to control future events.[18]

The *Zohar* describes the emergence of the ten sefirot from the "Ein Sof" (Endless or Infinite—also described as "nothingness," in terminology similar to Eastern philosophies). The first sefirah, now called Keter (Crown), is also called Ayin (Nothingness). It is envisaged as the crown on the head of the Adam Kadmon (as well as the head itself). The sefirot are also pictured as a "cosmic tree" growing downward from its root: Keter.

The *Zohar* introduces extensive mythical imagery with sexual symbolism when discussing the relationships among sefirot.

Keter emanates a "point," Hokmah (Wisdom), the second sefirah, now characterized as the Father. This point expands, forming Binah (Understanding), the womb, the divine Mother, who receives the seed of Hokmah. She conceives the seven lower sefirot in this order: Hesed (Love), Gevurah (Power—also the location of demonic and evil forces and also called Din, or Judgment), Tifaret (Beauty, also called Rahamim [Compassion] and Heaven, Sun, Son, King, Holy one, blessed be he); Netsach (Eternity), Hod (Splendor), Yesod (Foundation, also called Tsaddiq [Righteous One]). The light and power of all other sefirot are channeled through Yesod (seen as the male phallus) to Malkut/Shekinah (Presence or Kingdom). However, humans must enter the divine through Malkut/Shekinah.[19] According to Rabbi Joseph, a thirteenth-century kabbalist, Binah was considered the gentle, wise aspect of the feminine divine while Gevurah was the angry aspect. She was "red with anger" at being cut off from "her Lord." Her hair, like Adam Kadmon's beard, is black, curly, and oily, and is "alive with the power of destruction."[20]

What are we to make of this? In the description of Keter, we see a reversal in the Tree, for it now grows downward from its roots. To put it mildly, this is unnatural, and depicts the change from the Goddess symbol of a tree with its roots firmly planted in the earth, to a tree with its roots in transcendence.

Further, the undifferentiated light manifests first as the Supernal Father bearing the name (Hokmah/Wisdom) of a female manifestation of divinity. This "father," depicted as the active partner, impregnates (plants his seed in) the gentle, passive aspect of the female divine, specified here as the Mother Binah, the receptive partner, the receiving vessel. Gevurah is depicted as an uppity female. Her anger at being cut off from divinity, rather than being considered righteous or justified, becomes a source of evil or demonic powers. Though energies pass freely among other sefirot, Malkut/Shekinah can only receive from the sefirah above her, Yesod, the phallus. To put it bluntly, just as Binah's divinity comes only from receiving the male seed, so Malkut's divinity comes only through sexual intercourse with the male above her. However, at least one remnant of the Goddess's power remains: just as one enters earthly life through woman, so one can only enter the divine life through Malkut.

The implications of the *Zohar's* representation of the Godhead may go even further. According to Elliot Wolfson, the picture the *Zohar* presents is of a male androgynous godhead, whose male androgyny begins in the supposedly ungendered Ein Sof. (The term "male androgyny" means that the representation is male and phallic and that this male, phallic godhead contains feminine attributes.) Male androgynous symbolism extends to the act of creation, which in the *Zohar* becomes, in an act of male masturbation, God's writing or inscribing with his phallus in letters that are semen on a tablet understood to be feminine. Through this activity, God begets himself.[21]

This description is an example, par excellence, of reversal and attribution of Goddess traits to the male God. For in previous Goddess myths, the Goddess, complete unto herself (androgynous), orgasmically gives birth to the universe. She also gives birth to the male God, who in Kabbalah has found a way to circumvent the need to be born of woman.

In a commentary on the Genesis creation story, the Zohar says:

"The Beginning emanated, building itself a glorious palace. There it sowed the seed of holiness to give birth for the benefit of the universe. . . . The secret is 'With Beginning — created God.'"

The term "beginning" here refers to Hokmah, the father, and the "glorious palace" is Binah, the mother. Rather than accepting the biblical "in the beginning, God created. . ." the *Zohar*, in leaving the subject blank, turns it around. Matt's interpretation is that the great secret represented by the blank is that "an ineffable source" created God.[22]

Perhaps. But, at the very least, this is certainly an admission that "God" is not the original creator. One might be vague and call this original creator the "ineffable source," or one might be consistent with the facts of procreation and call her the Great Mother, the Goddess.

It is interesting to note here and keep in mind for a later discussion of language in chapter 5, that the *Zohar* is known to have given new meanings to words, some of which were incorrect translations of the original Hebrew and Aramaic. Also, the text often uses two different words to mean the same thing; this is most common with nouns.[23]

In the *Zohar*, Sabbath is personified as female, Shekinah—the Sabbath Queen, identified with the sefirah Malkut:

"When Sabbath enters she is alone, separated from the Other Side. . . Basking in the oneness of holy light, she is crowned over and over to face the holy king. . . . There is no power in all the worlds aside from her."

The "Other Side," here refers to the demonic realm which, according to kabbalistic thought, threatened both the Shekinah and her people on weekdays. The "holy king" is represented by the sefirah Tifaret.

In the *Zohar,* the Torah is personified as female, synonymously with Shekinah/Malkut. For example, "If this [perfect balance] is so with the angels, how much more so with Torah, who created them and all the worlds, and for whose sake they all exist. In descending to this world, if she did not put on the garments of this world, the world could not endure."[24]

Despite previously mentioned attempts to phallicize the Torah, it continued to be perceived by kabbalists as a crowned female wrapped in beautiful garments.[25] And to this day, "garments" cover the Torah scroll and the congregation rises to honor the Torah when the Ark opens to reveal her. Before the Torah can be read, her crown and garment—usually fringed, embellished, and embroidered velvet or silk—are removed. The two wooden legs of the scroll part as it is unrolled.

The *Zohar* relates that Shekinah, called the rainbow, "took off her garments and gave them to Moses. Wearing that garment he went up the mountain. . ." to receive the written commandments. "The garment" here becomes a cloud enclosing and protecting Moses.

Several interpretations may interest us. First, the rainbow here and in Genesis 9:13, and in Ezekiel 1:28 (where it is also enclosed in a cloud), are accepted as signs of the Shekinah. She is seen as manifesting a rainbow, representing the colors of all the sefirot.[26]

Second, Moses needs the blessing or power of the Shekinah in order to approach the male God—and in order to receive his written commandments. Through the Shekinah transferring her "rainbow" to Moses, and through Moses' going up on the mountain to receive his orders, power is transferred from the female to the male, both in the divine and earthly realms.

Further, the *Zohar* establishes a divinity with four aspects, composed of Father (Hokmah), Mother (Binah), Son/King (Tifaret) and Daughter (Malkut/Shekinah), also called by kabbalists Matronit or Matrona. Associated with these four aspects or persons were the four letters of the mystical divine name: YHVH. Y (in Hebrew, the letter yod) was the Father, H (in Hebrew, heh) the Mother (Binah). V (in Hebrew, vau), the Son, and the second H (heh), the daughter, were "crowned by their mother." The Shekinah, though the daughter, also had motherly traits and functioned as an intermediary between the people, or community of Israel, and God.[27]

The Hebrew letters of the divine name are said to reflect their maleness and femaleness, in part because of their shapes. In modern prayer books, the Hebrew word for YHVH is abbreviated by writing only two yods (the initial "male" letter). In any case, this word is never pronounced. (Considering the name of deity unpronounceable is another trait borrowed from the Goddess, one of whose epithets was "She whose name cannot be pronounced or spoken.") Rather, the Hebrew word "Adonai," meaning Lord, is substituted.

The *Zohar* description of the formation of its holy family includes a number of reversals. For example, Wisdom, called the Father, is said to have "spread out and brought forth" Understanding (that is, the Mother Binah). After the two unite, the Mother gives birth first to a son, and then to a daughter. The son is said to "nourish" the daughter.[28]

These passages are similar to other mythological descriptions of the female being born from the male, such as Eve from Adam's rib, and Athena from the brow of Zeus.

The four persons of the *Zohar* tetrad are similar to mythological tetrads of earlier cultures that include a father, mother, and two children, sometimes a son and daughter and sometimes two sons. Examples include: the Greek Cronus, Rhea, Zeus, and Hera; the Egyptian Shu (Father or sky god), Tefnut (Mother goddess of moisture), Geb (Son or Earth god), and Nut (daughter or sky goddess); the Indian Shiva/Rudha (Lord

of procreation and also lord of the dance), Parvati, the Great
mother, whose forms include Devi, Kali, and Shakti; Genesha
and Kartika; the Hittite/Canaanite Elkunirsa (or El, the male
creator, Ashertu (or Asherah, his wife), Baal-Hadad, their son,
and Ishtar (Astarte or Anath), their daughter; the Sumarian
An (god of heaven), Ninhursag (Great Mother, also called Ki
or Mother Earth), Enki (god of water) and Enlil (god of air).
It was from this last pantheon that the great Goddess Inanna
descended.

By the time these tetrads evolved in their respective cultures, it had become standard for the father god in some way
to "give birth" to the mother goddess. In addition, in cultures
where there was both a son and a daughter, the son was born
first. The son and daughter usually united sexually and in some
cultures the mother and father were also sister and brother.
Kabbalists rationalized their acceptance of the divine incest of
the son (Tifaret) and daughter (Shekinah/Malkut) by saying
that under the ideal circumstances of the divine realm, all
unions are permitted.[29]

In all cultures these tetrads represent transitions from previous matrifocal religions in which the Mother Goddess gave
birth to all—including the god (and any other children)—to
fully patriarchal religions in which deity is entirely male.

The mythology presented in the *Zohar* is of the same ilk,
but appears at a much later date than the actual transition. It
is likely, therefore, that it represents the writing down of an
oral tradition, passed down from generation to generation,
possibly combined with the familiarity of some kabbalists of
writings about these earlier mythologies.

For example, Patai credits the idea that God needs to be
united with his female counterpart in order to retain his power
to the influence of Indian beliefs about Shiva being incomplete without Shakti.[30] However, a clearer description of both

the kabbalistic and Indian expressions is that they are remnants
of earlier spiritual beliefs in the primacy of the female divine.

In part, Patai summarizes the central myth of zoharic
Kabbalah, as follows:

Adam's sin was that he mistook the tenth (and lowest)
sefirah (Malkut/Shekinah) for "the totality of the Godhead,"
which consisted of ten sefirot. This caused a break between
God and the Shekinah. Humanity continues to repeat Adam's
mistake, causing a continual separation between God and "his
spouse." The Shekinah became the Mother of Israel as well as
the representative (or intermediary) of the community of Israel before God. In addition, when the people of Israel sin, it
forces the divine couple to turn away from one another, allowing the forces of evil to attach themselves to the Shekinah, keeping her from union with God. When human husband and wife
have intercourse, it motivates the divine couple to do the same.[31]

But there is a further complication. The Temple at Jerusalem served as the bedchamber for God the King (Tifaret) and
the Shekinah, securing the well-being of Israel and the entire
world. When the Temple was destroyed, the Shekinah went
into exile with the community of Israel. This lessened God's
power. Since God can't get along without a female consort,
Shekinah's place was taken by Lilith, called "ruler of she-de-
mons." This situation will last until the Messiah comes and
enables the union of Shekinah with the King. At that time
Lilith will cease to exist.

To make things even more interesting, there is confusion
in the *Zohar* (as well as other kabbalistic literature) about
whether Lilith is separate from or the same as Shekinah. The
Zohar often refers to Lilith as "the slave-woman." In one instance, the *Zohar* says: "The Shekinah is at times called the
Mother, at times, the Slave-Woman, and at times the King's
Daughter." Another passage reads: "When Israel was exiled,

the Shekinah too went into exile, and this is the nakedness of the Shekinah. And this nakedness is Lilith. . . ."[32]

A CLEARER VISION

Seen in the light of current knowledge of Goddess religions, the myth central to Kabbalah begins with at least two reversals. First, the male God not only gives birth to the universe, but also has contractions in order to do so. This patriarchal reversal causes a separation between the divine and the physical world which had not previously existed. That is, because it is no longer a female deity who gives birth, the (male) divinity is forever separated from the creation (whereas in Goddess religions divinity is immanent in creation). Adam's sin is clearly Goddess worship—that is, understanding the whole of divinity as imaged as female. This concept is apparently a reversal of an earlier myth expressed in third-century gnosticism, in which the (biblical) male God mistakes himself for the entirety of divinity. According to this myth, a female divinity called Sophia "wanted to create something, alone without her consort. . . ." Her creation was an imperfect male God who "became arrogant, saying 'It is I who am God, and there is none other apart from me.' When he said this, he sinned against the entirety."[33]

Regarding the Jerusalem Temple, it is known that the Goddess (as Asherah and in other forms) was worshipped there, with King Solomon one of her devotees.[34] When the Temple was destroyed, so was the home of the Goddess and her consort, and thus divinity was weakened by victorious patriarchy. She was absent, separated out of divinity, not by some mystical, mythological event, but by human actions to suppress her worship.

The union of God the King with Lilith can be seen from several different perspectives. First, characterizing Lilith as a she-demon is a way of saying that the present concept of divinity is not only less than perfect, but perverse. Second, the use of the female divinity Lilith to represent this imperfection, this perversity, represents the demonization both of the Goddess and of women, and the separation of women into the categories of "good" and "evil." Third, the confusion over whether Shekinah and Lilith are separate or identical reflects men's ambivalence towards women. Further, the inclusion of Lilith could be seen as a persistence of the trinity of maiden, mother, and crone, with Malkut functioning as the triune Goddess (Shekinah=Maiden, Matronit=Mother, Lilith=Crone). However, because the natural cycle has been obliterated, the crone (Lilith) can only be perceived as evil.

The myth of the reunion of the Shekinah with the male god is in reality a yearning for the return of the Goddess to divinity—for the acceptance of the female divine, not just as the female part of the male, but as a full equal. When this happens, Lilith will not cease to be, rather she and Shekinah will again be understood to be two aspects of the Goddess. And we, too, will be whole. This happens not with the coming of the Messiah—spiritual leadership vested in one man—but with the coming of what I suggest calling the Age of Perfection or the Age of Bliss—when all participate equally in spirit.

The Age of Bliss comes when mother is no longer divided against daughter, nor sister against sister, and when female and male are united in true equality in our perception of the divine and in our everyday lives.

Chapter 3
Kabbalah: From Spain to Safed

Wisdom spreads over all created things: mineral, vegetable, animal, and human. Do not uproot anything that grows, unless it is necessary. Do not kill any living creature, unless it is necessary.

— Moses Cordovero, sixteenth-century kabbalist

...supernal holiness does not abide with anyone attached by even a hair to the material realm.

—Hayyim Vital, Lurianic kabbalist, seventeenth century

↜ KABBALAH REMAINED RELATIVELY ESOTERIC, known in only limited circles, until after 1492, when the Jews were expelled from Spain as part of the Inquisition—that same madness that brought the burning of millions of Europeans (mostly women) accused of witchcraft.

During that tumultuous time, many people believed the end of the world was at hand and the Messiah was coming. These beliefs became an important part of Kabbalah, attracting more people to it.

By the 1530s, Safed, a town in what was then Palestine and to which many of the Spanish Jews fled, became the new center of kabbalistic thinking. What had previously been simply mystical thoughts, ideas, theories, and philosophies became ritualized in Safed during the sixteenth and early seventeenth centuries.

For example, one of the rituals of Safed kabbalists—all men—was the welcoming of the Sabbath Queen. The men went out into the fields on Fridays just before sunset to welcome the Shekinah. They wrote a song, called "Lekha Dodi," which is still sung in on Friday nights in synagogues worldwide:

Come, let us go meet the Sabbath,
For she is the source of blessing,
Pouring forth from ancient days.
The act was the end, in thought the beginning. . . .
Awake, awake for your light has come!. . .
And the City will be rebuilt on her mound. . .
Come in peace, O crown of her husband. . . .
Come, O Bride, come, O Bride![1]

The Safed field where this celebration took place came to be called the sacred pomegranate (or apple) orchard and the fields themselves came to be considered a manifestation of the Shekinah, one of whose epithets became "the orchard." This Sabbath celebration is similar to customs in cultures honoring the Teutonic Goddess Frigga—whose name means Friday—and the Middle Eastern Goddess Ishtar, whose symbol was the evening star (Venus).

After the celebration in the fields, the men went to evening prayers at the synagogue. Each man then returned home, where his wife had a meal ready for the family. Before the meal, the man would sing praises to the "woman of valor," using the text of Proverbs 31. The "woman of valor" was understood to be both his wife and the Shekinah. This chant is still sung in Jewish homes at Sabbath observances. Sex was not allowed on Friday evening, but at midnight it was considered incumbent upon the kabbalistic man to have sex with his wife. Because on Sabbath she was the earthly representative of the Shekinah, this coitus was a sacred act.[2]

CORDOVERO'S CONCEPTS

The Safed mystic considered by many to be the most important kabbalistic thinker, Moses Cordovero (b. 1522), completed his main work, *The Pomegranate Orchard (Pardes Rimmomim)*, by his twenty-seventh birthday, so apparently the proscription against kabbalistic work before the age of forty did not apply to him. But, of course, women were still not allowed to participate, except as needed by the men, as Sabbath stand-ins for the Shekinah.

Cordovero's aim was to unify the concept of God's transcendence as represented by the kabbalistic concept of the Ein Sof, with what he considered the more personal or immanent divine concept represented by the sefirot. Cordovero taught that the sefirot were beings emanated from God and that God was immanent in them; that the sefirot were tools for God, vessels containing the "divine substance."[3]

Regarding the Ein Sof, Cordovero wrote:

"Before anything emanated, there was only Ein Sof. . . . Similarly, after it brought into being that which exists, there is nothing but it. You cannot find anything that exists apart from it. There is nothing that is not pervaded by the power of divinity. . . . Everything is within it; it is within everything and outside of everything. There is nothing but it."[4]

Cordovero and others sometimes spoke in terms of three roots, or lights (also called "splendors") which were sometimes understood to be located above the Tree, in the area of the Ein Sof, and sometimes understood to be emanating through Keter, Hokmah, and Binah. These additions were probably made so the Tree would conform with the Jewish belief that God had thirteen attributes. [5]

In describing the relation of Ein Sof to the sefirot, Cordovero calls Ein Sof the "cause of causes," the "one that cannot be counted" (referring to the literal meaning of sefirot as that which can be counted).

He continues:

"Ein Sof emanated its sefirot, through which its actions are performed. They serve as vessels for the actions. . . in the world of separation and below. . . . These qualities possess unerasable names. . . ."[6]

The names are called "unerasable" because they are so holy that, once written, they may not be erased. The unerasable names are Eheyah (I am), Yah (an abbreviation of YHVH), YHVH, Elohim, El, Tseva'ot, Shaddai, El Chai, and Adonai. They were attached to the various "qualities," that is, sefirot, as shown in the chart at the end of this chapter. Cordovero taught "these names are the sefirot," not merely ascribed to the sefirot. That is, the sefirot and the holy name were considered one and inseparable.

The name, "I am," attached to Keter, comes from the words the Bible attributes to God when he (sic) reveals himself to Moses at the burning bush, traditionally translated: "I am that I am."

The name Yah, connected to Hokmah, is half of the divine name (YHVH) associated with God the King (Tifaret) here. As attached to the supernal father, the name is an abbreviation containing only the half considered masculine. (What was considered to be the feminine half, VEH [sometimes transliterated WEH], was associated with the female sefirot Malkut.)[7]

Yet Binah, the supernal mother, has the full divine name YHVH, containing both male and female. This interpretation is strengthened by Binah's second holy name, Elohim, which is a plural noun for divinity that includes both female and male. Hesed's "El" is the masculine singular of the latter. Again Gevurah, which in one kabbalistic light flow receives light from Binah, is also named Elohim. Tifaret, like Binah, has the name YHVH. Netsach and Hod have the name "Tseva'ot" (Lord of

Hosts). Yesod is called El Shaddai, a male-god name that also is the noun (still male!) for female breasts. Yesod is also called El Chai, the living God or God of life. Since Yesod also represents the male phallus, one may speculate here on the sexual confusion of phalluses and breasts. The sex change of "shaddai" (breast) into a male noun is no doubt another instance of a potent feminine symbol being appropriated by patriarchy.[8] In addition, the source of life (El Chai) is here attributed to the penis, rather than the womb (an epithet of Binah).

In Kabbalah of the sixteenth century, Adonai was considered to have a feminine connotation, and Yahweh, a masculine one. This explains the assignment of the divine name Adonai to Malkut, despite Adonai's translation as "Lord."[9]

Cordovero says that "Ein Sof is not identical with Keter," as other kabbalists had suggested. Rather, he insists, "Ein Sof is the cause of Keter. . . From Keter the rest of the emanation is drawn forth. . . . "

However, Keter does not "reveal itself," rather it is known through Da'at (Knowledge), a sefirah located between Binah and Hokmah and often not included in the drawing of the Tree. What this means is that Keter (a masculine noun) and Da'at (a feminine noun) are synonymous, but we cannot know Keter directly, we can only know Keter through our perception of Da'at. [10]

According to Cordovero, the ten sefirot are "souls" which "clothe themselves" in "names" which "serve as vessels for the ten essences:

"Before the qualities emanated they were utterly concealed within Ein Sof, united with it. . . . Afterward Ein Sof emanated one point from itself. . . . Keter, called Ayin, Nothingness. . . ." The second point, Cordovero continues, was Hokmah and the third, Binah. "From these three sefirot emerged the six dimensions of providence." Separate from the six, the last, Malkut, Cordovero says, "is the entirety."

Cordovero gives three examples of how this emanation took place which, he says, should be understood to have no particular order (that is, none preceded another nor is one more important than another). He also says that sefirot should be understood to have "no specific location."[11]

We can see then, persisting into the picture that Cordovero presents, the idea of divine immanence and an attempt at asserting a nonhierarchical divine scheme.

Cordovero describes channels, or "paths of the ray of illumination," through which the divine light travels. He asserts that the channels are innumerable and then gives one example.

In this example, the light has several possible routes as it travels through the sefirot. However, there is only one route, or path, to Malkut: "Malkut receives solely from Yesod, through whom she receives them all. Without him, she cannot receive any of them; without her, none of the sefirot can emanate to the lower worlds, for she is the essence of those worlds, conducting them. . .each sefirah acts only with all the others, with their consent, through Malkut."[12]

Again we are told that Malkut/Shekinah, at the end of the divine line, can receive divine illumination only from the male/phallus Yesod. She is seen as receiving divine light from Yesod— as being part of divinity—but also as being the essence of the "lower worlds," that is the material world: Earth. She is the link between the divine and substance, which here have become separate. Because of her closeness to substance she cannot partake as totally and independently of the divine. In this depiction, female divinity has become fully receptive and dependent on male divinity for her power. Yet she still retains the remnants of her former power in the perception that all sefirot act together through her so that in some way she still represents "the entirety" of all the sefirot.

Although Cordovero seems to argue against hierarchy, he nevertheless proposes several, the flow of divine emanation being one, and the proscription against probing "the essence of the first three sefirot," being another. In this instance, Keter is called "Divine Mind," not its usual epithet but an influential one, especially in later Qabalah and other theosophies, and in the idea that mind is higher than and separate from the physical body. Further, Cordovero says, "It is also improper to probe the essence of hidden substance that creates all that exists. . . . However, it is not wrong for us to explore from Hesed and Gevurah on down."

Nevertheless, Cordovero assigned colors to the first three sefirot, as well as the second three, and in doing so offered further explanations of their nature.

Keter, he said, has three colors, demonstrating its three aspects: black, "by virtue of being the emanator," (that is, black represents the nothingness from which it emanates); no color, "because it is not revealed to what is emanated," (that is, what is emanated is revealed not through Keter but only through Da'at); and white, representing compassion it emanates to the other sefirot.

The color of Hokmah is blue or blue-black, like the color of sapphires, "the first color to emerge out of black." Binah's color is green "like grass," because this color contains the colors of Hokmah, Hesed, Gevurah, and Tifaret showing that "all these qualities blend together in Binah."

Hesed's color is white, denoting virtue and love. But the type of love it represents, Cordovero makes clear, is free of contamination of sexual arousal located in Gevurah, whose color is red and is on "the left." This purified love, located on "the right" draws the person toward Hokmah, the sefirah above it. Hesed nullifies "the power of aliens" located to its left, in Gevurah.

The red of Gevurah represents harsh judgement, discipline, and "aliens that seduce and denounce, terror, the arousal of love" (we might say lust), and wealth. Yet, "every time God listens to a prayer or cry of distress, it is through this quality, with the help of Binah."

Tifaret's colors are white and red and also topaz yellow. His epithets are beauty and splendor and souls emanate from him, through his union with Malkut.

Cordovero says: "Such union takes place between these two sefirot as well as Hokmah and Binah, but between none of the others."[13]

What are we to make of these colors and their corresponding traits? We can wonder at the triplicity of colors in Keter, two of which (black and white) are two of the colors of the triple Goddess (the third is red).

The color of sapphire blue for Hokmah reinforces its primacy since it is perceived as close to the black of Keter's nothingness. The color green for Binah, especially in its derivation from the color of the grass, appears to be a remnant of Earth religions, which see their deity immanent in Earth, including the grasses of her fields. It is a tie-in with Malkut, who in this scheme is not assigned a color. Whether green contains all the other colors could be argued, as green is actually composed of the primary colors blue and yellow. However, this blending of colors in Binah emphasizes the importance of the supernal mother, who contains all, including Hokmah, from whom she supposedly emanates!

The explanations of Hesed and Gevurah come from the view that the Hesed, vertically below Hokmah, is related to its maleness and they are "on the right"; Gevurah, vertically below Binah, is related to its femaleness and they are "on the left."

The associations of "left" at this time included female and evil—part of the demonization of women and the Goddess, who is also associated with the left. The associations of the "right" were male and, of course, virtue. The problem that in contemporary times is often phrased "If God is good and all is God how can evil exist?" is solved here by accepting that "aliens that seduce and denounce" are nevertheless part of the Godhead; they are located in a part of divinity that is feminine. And they are located in the same area as lust—both for sex and for money. In other words, added to the supernal mother's (Binah's) receptiveness is the location of all negative qualities in the feminine. Yet to get access to God, our prayer or "cry of distress" must travel first through this negative area; only then, with the Mother (Binah) as intermediary, does it finally gets to the ear of "God."

Tifaret, he of the red and the white, mediates and is the product of the types of love in both Hesed and Gevurah, since he is the son of Hokmah and Binah, the product of a sexual union requiring both arousal and virtuous love. In turn, he enjoys sexual union with Malkut, the daughter of Hokmah and Binah. However, in another reversal, it is he, not Malkut, who gives birth, in this instance to souls, which derive from Binah.

Other epithets Cordovero used for the sefirot continue the sexual description, which he takes pains to assure us is meta- phor. Tifaret and Malkut are called the groom and bride, lower father and mother, son and daughter, king and queen, and the Holy One, blessed be he, and the Shekinah. Hesed and Gevurah help in the arousal of love, through sexual foreplay, through "the kiss. . .the mystery of the mouth, Malkut being in Tifaret, Tifaret in Malkut." ("The mouth" is an epithet of Malkut/Shekinah.) Netsach and Hod are understood to be the testicles of the Adam Kadmon and Yesod, the penis, called rather coyly "the mystery of the covenant."[14] In other words, all sefirot but the first three are involved in aiding the union of Tifaret and Malkut.

In another doctrine that was later adopted by the Western esoteric tradition, Cordovero describes the balance of polari- ties or extremes within the Tree. In this view, the sefirot on the right are seen as opposites of those on the left with those in the middle moderating, or mediating the two extremes. Tifaret, "in the mystery of Da'at" (previously described as the outward Keter) balances the extremes of the female Binah and the male Hokmah. Tifaret, in this instance called by his other name, Rahamim (Compassion) mediates or balances the polarities of the masculine Hesed, pure love, and the feminine Gevurah, pure lust, judgement, and home of a host of unsavory characters. In these two triangles, male and female are seen as opposite polarities that need balancing (rather than as complements that can work in partnership). Further, all passive and negative qualities are assigned to the feminine polarities, while the masculine are seen as active and positive.

Netsach and Yod, the two testicles, are "balanced" by Yesod, the penis. Thus, as in biology, that which is produced in Netsach and Yod, is brought into Yesod for ejaculation into Malkut, keeping the "balance" in the testicles.

Cordovero also presents four divisions of divine existence. All sefirot are present in all four divine worlds, but in different ways. In the world called "Atzilut," (a noun usually translated Emanation, but also having the meaning of aristocracy and which can be both masculine and feminine) the ten sefirot are emanations from the Ein Sof.

In the division called Beriah (usually translated Creation, but a feminine noun meaning creature), the light of the Ein Sof is clothed in the various qualities or essences of the sefirot. In addition, this is called the "Realm of the Throne of Glory." ("Throne" is one of the epithets of the sefirah Malkut.)

In the third division, Yetsirah (usually called formation, but also a feminine noun meaning creation), the emanated light of the sefirot takes form, and the most important of those forms found here are ten bands of angels and the celestial palaces.

The fourth division is Assiyah (usually translated actualization but also a feminine noun that means action). Here the sefirot shine through ten heavens. "Here, holiness pervades physical matter."[15]

Cordovero, in a further elaboration of the Holy name YHVH, says that it comprises all ten sefirot. However, Y means Hokmah, the first H Binah, V the six following sefirot, and the second H Malkut.

Cordovero discusses how a man could become "a vehicle" for the sefirot and aid in the unification of Tifaret and Malkut. To accomplish reunification, Cordovero instructs kabbalists "to pray. . .to unite the Blessed Holy One [Tifaret] and Shekinah." In this view, the goal of all prayer and of following religious requirements is to unite "the masculine and feminine halves of divinity."[16]

LURIANIC KABBALAH

Cordovero's teachings were made more rigid and, in some cases, entirely changed (some might say distorted) in the teachings of Isaac Luria Ashkenazi (1534-1572) usually called by his first two names only and referred to as "the sacred lion" from the acronym (Ari) of his Hebrew names.

Though an enormously influential teacher, Luria preferred not to write, and his teachings are known mainly through the prolific writings of one of his students, Hayyim Vital (1542-1620).

Lurianic Kabbalah focuses on meditation involving letter combinations, and on creation theory associated with the mystical use of language and holy names.

Luria departed greatly from Cordovero and other kabbalists who held in common (despite a wide variety of embellishments and elaborations) the basic concept that Ein Sof progressively emanates through creation in continuous stages;

that is, Ein Sof and the emanations are closely bound together. Lurianic Kabbalah, on the other hand, "created an enormous chasm between Ein Sof and the world of emanation. . . ." and filled the world of emanation with "divine acts of which the earlier Kabbalah had known nothing."[17]

Luria elevated to the level of doctrine two previous kabbalistic ideas: contraction (in Hebrew, zimzum) and reunification through prayer and concentration (kavannah). He emphasized the importance of special reunification prayers, called in Hebrew, yehudim. In addition, he added a doctrine called "breaking of the vessels" (shiverah), that effectively separated spirit from matter.

Contraction, according to Luria, occurred: "At the beginning of creation, when Ein Sof withdrew its presence all around in every direction, it left a vacuum in the middle, surrounded on all sides by the light of Ein Sof."[18]

In other words, in order for creation to occur, God had to withdraw, or become smaller, so that something other than God could exist.

This view is in stark contrast to that of preceding kabbalists. For example, Cordovero, who also speaks of "the contraction of God's presence," clarifies that "nothing is outside of God. This applies not only to the sefirot, but to everything that exists. . . they exist through the divine energy that flow through them and clothes itself in them."[19] Luria's doctrine, however, presents a separation of divinity from creation—a separation of the creator from the created.

Before Luria, "contraction" meant a concentration of God's power in a specific place. In Lurianic doctrine it takes on the opposite meaning of withdrawal from a place.[20]

The meaning of "zimzum" is then changed from the feminine birth contraction—which can certainly be described as a concentration of power—to withdrawal, a masculine action that immediately follows the procreative act. With this change from femalelike to malelike creation, any chance of divine immanence is lost. God becomes fully transcendent and creation and the created become not-of-God (not divine).

But Luria did not stop there. He maintained that Malkut/Shekinah became male when exposed either to human males or the male sefirot. It is this transformation into maleness that empowers her and endows her with the godname, Adonai.[21] Further, Luria's doctrine of the breaking of the vessels widens the chasm between the creator and the creation. Comparing the sefirot to a potter's unformed mass of clay, Vital renders Luria's teaching:

"As this light began to enter the mass, vessels were formed. From the purest light, Keter; next, Hokmah; then Binah; and so on through all ten sefirot. Since Keter was the purest and clearest of all the vessels, it could bear the light within it. . . but Hokmah and Binah. . . . their backs broke, and they fell from their position. As the light descended further six points appeared—six fragments of what had been one point of light. Thus the vessels shattered. Their spiritual essence—the light—ascended back to the mother's womb [Binah], while the shattered vessels fell to the world of creation."[22]

Since the emanations can be understood as the overflow ejaculation from the male God's act of creation, and the vessels represent the receiving female(s),[23] the implication is that the female is inadequate, unable to contain the male "emanations." Or perhaps what we have here is a case of cosmic rape, in which the female is improperly prepared, or unwilling! In any case, the cosmic catastrophe then becomes the fault of the inadequate, unwilling unsubmissive female vessels.

After this cosmic catastrophe, which according to Luria was part of the divine plan, creation was entirely changed. The first form of emanation after the withdrawal became not Keter but the Adam Kadmon (primordial man). Luria introduced the concept that Adam Kadmon is a realm above the worlds beginning with Azilut, and that the supernal lights emanate from Adam Kadmon. The primordial man thus becomes an intermediary between Ein Sof and the rest of creation—the hierarchy of sefirot and other worlds. In fact, in Lurianic Kabbalah, Ein Sof and Adam Kadmon are sometimes used synonymously.[24]

According to Luria, tremendous lights radiated from the head of the Adam Kadmon, some taking the form of letters, thus joining the symbolism of light and language. These light/letters combined to form sacred names.

All lights emanating from the Adam Kadmon were given vessels. The three upper vessels were able to contain the light which flowed first through Keter, then Hokmah, then Binah. But the light that emanated from Binah reached the lower six vessels (Hesed through Yesod) all at once and the force of the light broke them. Malkut cracked, we are told, but did not break to the same degree as the previous six.

Some of the light retraced its path back to its source (Binah). The rest of the light was "hurled down" with the shards of the vessels and from this "dark forces. . . took on substance." In addition to being the source of evil, the shards are also the source of "gross matter."[25]

Thus, according to Lurianic doctrine, not only is the material world—Earth and all its physical substance including human life—not-of-God, it also comes from the same source as evil.

Whether explaining the breaking of the vessels as caused by the weakness of the vessels, or as being intentionally broken by the Godhead to make way for punishment and retribution[26] or as resulting from Adam's sin of contemplating only the last sefirah (Malkut) rather than all of them, or as a result of cosmic rape, the outcome of the catastrophe is the same—the banishment of the female from divinity.

For we are told that the pressure of the light caused Hokmah and Binah, as well as the four worlds of Atzilut, Beriah, Yetsirah, and Assiyah—which in Lurianic Kabbalah were ranked one above the other—to descend one level from their original places. Malkut/Shekinah was therefore exiled from the rest of divinity and partakes of the contaminated material world.

This then can be seen as a metaphor for the patriarchal process: divinity is no longer immanent, spirit is separated from matter, the physical world is seen as tarnished (if not evil), and the female is no longer part of divinity.

But another truth is also intimated: that this description represents an imperfect version of both creation and divinity.

The third Lurianic doctrine, therefore, is an attempt to perfect divinity. This cosmic restoration and reintegration, (in Hebrew, tikkun), is to be brought about by the action of the lights emanating from the head of the Adam Kadmon, which have the ability to reorganize disheveled divinity. To accomplish this male reorganization project, "faces" (in Hebrew, parzufim) take the place of the sefirot. Keter is reformed into "the long-faced one" or "ancient one" and the image of an old man with a beard replaces what had been an abstract and genderless sefirah. Hokmah and Binah are reformed into "faces" with the Hebrew names Abba (father) and Imma (mother). Their union serves as an archetype for the procreative process which is called "looking face to face." The sparks from the broken vessels which have returned to Binah/Imma increase her receptivity so that coupling can take place. These assisting sparks are called "the female waters."

From the union of Abba and Imma is born a son, "the short-faced one," which comprises the six lower sefirot from Hesed to Yesod; the sefirot that previously had trouble con-

taining the light are now formed into one male personification. This son has been developed from an embryo in Imma,
who gives birth to and nurses him. Malkut becomes a "face"
called "the female of the short-faced one" and is considered
the feminine complement of the "short-faced one."[27]

She has two facets or "persons": Leah and Rachel, named
after the biblical matriarchs. In his relationship with Malkut,
the "short-faced one" is called Jacob or Israel. On weekdays,
Jacob/Israel has sex with Leah. Considered the lower facet of
the Shekinah, Leah reaches only to the short-faced one's chest.
At midnight Friday until the end of the Sabbath, Jacob/Israel
copulates with Rachel. Considered the higher facet of the
Shekinah, she occupies a "face-to-face" position with the short-
faced one during intercourse.[28]

Lurianic Kabbalah presents five parts of divinity where previously there were ten parts. These parts are more fully personified into humanlike "faces."

Atzilut is now called "The World of Balance." The three
other worlds retain their names and are now considered "lower."
Reinforcing this hierarchy, is a curtain at the bottom of each
world to filter out light that should stay at that level and go no
lower.

This reorganization, according to Luria, restores much of
divinity, yet it is still not perfect. The job of perfecting it further falls to humans, and it is the completion of this perfection that is the aim of religious activity.

Specifically the goal of Lurianic Kabbalah is overcoming
the historic exile of the Jewish people and the mystic exile of
the Shekinah, which are understood to be linked.[29]

To accomplish this Luria expanded and made more dog-
matic Cordovero's concepts of concentration (kavannah) and
reunifications (yehudim). Luria taught that when performing
any religious act, the man must concentrate on one purpose:

the reunification of the short-faced one (also called by the same epithets as Tiferet) and female-of-the-short-faced-one (also called Malkut/Shekinah). This reunification also brings about union of Binah/Imma and Hokmah/Abba.

A typical statement prefacing prayer was: "For the unification of the Holy One, blessed be He, and His Shekinah, in fear and love, to unite the YaH with the WeH in a complete union, in the name of all Israel, and to raise up the Shekinah from the dust. . ."[30]

Wolfson contends that this reunification is not the union of two equals, but rather the reabsorption of the female into the male godhead. By this action, the femaleness of the Shekinah is overcome,[31] in a way similar to that suggested by the Gnostic Gospel of Thomas, which attributes to Jesus these words: ". . .every woman who will make herself male will enter the Kingdom of heaven." [32]

Luria's scribe, Vital, gave these instructions for accomplishing "reunification":

"Strip your body from your soul, as if you do not feel that you are clothed in matter at all—you are entirely soul. The more you strip yourself of material being, the more powerful your comprehension. . . . if you do not train yourself to completely strip your soul from your body, the spirit will not rest upon you. . . .pray this prayer with perfect intention. . . . making yourself into a throne for the divine presence, your body an ark for Shekinah."[33]

Lurianic Kabbalah completes the separation of spirit and matter. Spirit cannot enter a person unless he (again, these were acts and prayers limited to men) completely detaches himself from the material, the physical—including of course the diversion of human female presence. Only when he is emptied of the physical—only when he is separated from his body—can he act as a vehicle—or stand in for the male God—in the reintegration of the Shekinah into divinity. In detaching himself from the material world, he experiences union with the feminine divine and through experiencing this union, he enables a similar uniting of the Shekinah and the male God. But this can be seen not as a union of equals, but rather as an absorption of the female into the male.

Thus, Kabbalah, taken to its extreme but logical conclusion under patriarchy, succeeds in separating body from spirit and matter from divinity, exiles the feminine from divinity—allowing her to return only if masculinized—and provides a theological rationale for why women (who are limited to passively representing the Shekinah to sanctify sex) cannot participate on the same full, active—and intellectual—level as men in the reunification.

Unfortunately, it is Lurianic Kabbalah, rather than earlier more immanent, less misogynist versions, that became incorporated into the form of Western mysticism its adherents call Qabalah.

Cordovero's Correspondences

Quality (sefirah)	Uneraseable Name	Color
Keter (Crown)	Eheyeh (I am)	black none white
Hokmah (Wisdom)	Yah (short for YHVH)	sapphire-blue
Binah (Understanding)	YHVH/Elohim (male/female deity)	green
Hesed (Love)	El (male deity)	white
Gevurah (Power)	Elohim (male/female deities)	red
Tifaret (Beauty)	YHVH	white & red (also topaz)
Netsach (Eternity)	Tseva'ot (Lord of hosts)	
Hod (Splendor)	Tseva'ot (Lord of hosts)	
Yesod (Foundation)	El Shaddai (eternal;literally breasted deity) El Hai (powerful; literally God of life)	
Malkut (Kingdom)	Adonai (Lord)	

QABALAH TREE

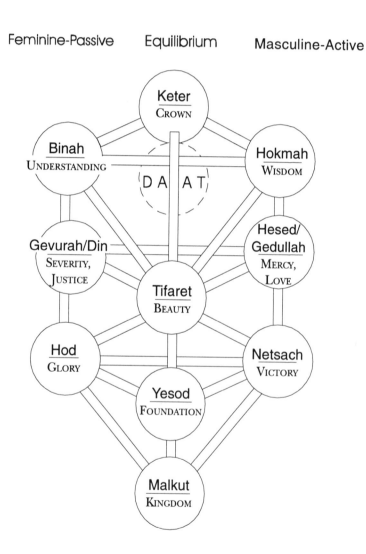

Feminine-Passive   Equilibrium   Masculine-Active

Keter
CROWN

Binah
UNDERSTANDING

DAAT

Hokmah
WISDOM

Hesed/
Gedullah
MERCY,
LOVE

Gevurah/Din
SEVERITY,
JUSTICE

Tifaret
BEAUTY

Hod
GLORY

Netsach
VICTORY

Yesod
FOUNDATION

Malkut
KINGDOM

Chapter 4
Qabalah

A goddessless religion is half-way to atheism.

—Dion Fortune, 1935

↩ QABALAH IS THE BASIS of the Western mystical or "mystery" tradition, also called the Western esoteric tradition. It incorporates many kabbalistic beliefs, plus material from other traditions. In the Order of the Golden Dawn, which flourished in the late nineteenth and early twentieth centuries in Great Britain and to a lesser extent continental Europe and the United States, Qabalah took its most dramatic and well-known form. Out of Golden Dawn came several writers and teachers—among them Arthur E. Waite, Aleister Crowley, and Dion Fortune—whose teachings continue to influence many metaphysical and psychic organizations today. Other Golden Dawn members, many of whom were involved in literature and the theater, included the poet William Butler Yeats; Maude Gonne, an Irish nationalist activist involved in a "spiritual union" with Yeats; and Mina (who changed her name to Moina) Bergson, an artist whose brother was French philosopher Henri Bergson and whose husband was Samuel L. "MacGregor" Mathers, Golden Dawn dictatorial leader.

The Golden Dawn grew out of Rosicrucianism and Masonic Lodges of the 1800s. One motivation for its formation may have been the inclusion of women, who were banned from the lodges.[1] Emerging from the Victorian era, several of the Golden Dawn members espoused various feminist causes of the day.[2]

The beliefs of the Golden Dawn were a pastiche of Jewish Kabbalah, which formed its main focus, Egyptian and Greek traditions and deities, and Christianity. Their practices were interwoven with the use and symbolism of Tarot, a deck of seventy-eight illustrated cards.[3] In addition, parts of the order's rituals appear similar to today's Wiccan practices.

Despite this amalgam of unorthodox traditions, the Golden Dawn was extremely hierarchical and authoritarian. Its members pledged secrecy upon pain of death.

Happily for us, Golden Dawn members—in particular Crowley, Fortune, and Waite—broke this pledge after becoming disillusioned with the order. Both Fortune and Crowley claimed to be targets of psychic attack as a result of revealing the order's secrets.

The Golden Dawn was at its strongest in Great Britain from 1888, when it was founded, to about 1892, when Moina and MacGregor Mathers moved to Paris. After this time, disagreements between the authoritarian MacGregor and other members, as well as among nonmembers—caused rifts and schism. The coup de grace was delivered by a scandal involving a couple on the fringes of the order, who, under the pretense of performing Golden Dawn rituals, raped a young girl. Though the Golden Dawn did not condone, let alone conduct rituals involving such actions, the newspapers connected the ritual rape to the order, weakening further an already weakened organization.[4]

Though the Golden Dawn continued after this time (indeed it still exists today), it never regained the status and strength of its earlier days. Yet the Golden Dawn of the late 1800s and early 1900s remains the most influential single organization in its impact on today's mystical/magical practice and thought.

BEFORE THE DAWN

In addition to the general influences of Rosicrucianism and Freemasonry, a more specific influence on the Golden Dawn was the work of the Eliphas Lévi, the "Hebrew" name assumed by Frenchman Alphonse-Louis Constant (1810-1875). A former Benedictine monk in rebellion against the church, Lévi studied Jewish Kabbalah, and added Roman Catholic and other Christian concepts, and included material on Tarot.

In his book *Le Livre des Splendours* (published in English by Weiser in 1973 as *The Book of Splendours*), Lévi presents his version of the *Zohar*, including his commentary on it. For example, his translation of one zoharic text reads:

"Woman does not possess within herself strength and justice, these she must receive from man. She aspires after them with untellable thirst, but cannot receive them until she is entirely submissive. When she rules, she brings about only revolt and violence. It is in this way that woman became man's overseer by drawing him into sin. In the incontinence of her desires, she became a mother and gave birth to Cain. Then she said: 'God and I have made a man, and this man is my property.'

"She was not yet ready for true maternity, for the serpent had infected her with his jealousy and anger. The birth of the cruel and pitiless Cain was a violent and terrible one, exhausting all the energies of woman. She grew softer then, weaker, and brought forth the gentle Abel. . . .

"Happy are the souls who descend in a direct line from the great Adam! For the children of the useless Abel and those of the criminal Cain are no better than the others: they are the unjust, the sinners."[5]

This text, consistent with Lévi's Paulist training, clearly states several misogynist themes common to Christianity of that time and to Lurianic Kabbalah:

- 🏵 women are meant to be weak, both mentally and physically
- 🏵 when women are not submissive, catastrophe ensues
- 🏵 woman's sexual desire tarnishes divinity, and therefore ancestry is better traced to a man (in this case, Adam), rather than to birth through a woman.

Lévi's book also contains a section on "Christian Glory," an extensive discussion of Satan and other "fallen angels," and a section called "Legend of Krishna," in which Lévi equates the story of Jesus with Hindu mythology. He also presents ten lessons on Qabalah with such typical reversal statements as: "Man is the son of woman, but woman comes out of man as number comes out of unity."[6]

THE GOLDEN DAWN

While incorporating some of Lévi's philosophy, the Order of the Golden Dawn added an enormous amount in formulating rituals, codifying concepts, and incorporating material from other spiritual traditions.

Taking its name from rituals supposedly performed in Egypt during the reign of Rameses II (about 1400 B.C.E.), but probably written by Mathers[7] with Moina's help,[8] the Golden Dawn used the kabbalistic Tree in a way it had never been used in Judaism: as a model for its organizational hierarchy. The order retained the concept of creation emanating from the top of the Tree down, but in practical use, the Tree was climbed from the bottom (Malkut) up. Though we might hope this signaled a more naturalistic concept of the Tree glyph, such was not the intent. Rather, its meaning was that the person ignorant of mystic truth has to start at the bottom of the ladder, which is matter—the material world.

Each path, each sefirah, was seen as a step up to a spirituality that looked with disdain on Earth and on matter. The neophyte, the person just joining the order, was considered not to be on the Tree at all. Not until the person studied the names and alchemical symbols of the four elements (earth, air, fire, and water), the signs of the zodiac and their relation to the four elements and other astrological information, and the Hebrew alphabet, could the member be admitted to the lowest sefirah, Malkut, in the rank the order called "Zelator." Other ranks of what was called the "Outer Order" (encompassing sefirot Malkut to Netsach) had similar study requirements. In passing from one grade to another, the member was considered to be moving or progressing on the paths connecting the sefirot. To these paths were assigned the twenty-two major arcana cards of the Tarot. The "minor arcana" cards in four suits were assigned to the sefirot.

The "Inner Order" or "Second Order" began in Tifaret and extended through Hesed. Its rituals revolved around the Rosicrucian legend of the death and resurrection of "Christian Rosenkreutz." The "Invisible" or "Third" Order, encompassing the sefirot Binah, Hokmah, and Keter, was the domain of the "Secret Chiefs" who supposedly guided the order and from whom Mathers said he received his directions.[9]

Thus the Tree became a strict hierarchy whose orders came from the top and which the individual ascended from the bottom.

After Zelator, the other ranks, apparently taken from Rosicrucian tradition, and their corresponding sefirot were: Theoreticus, Yesod; Practicus, Hod; Philosophus, Netsach; Adeptus Minor, Tifaret; Adeptus Major, Gevurah; Adeptus Exemplus, Hesed; Magester Templi, Binah; Magus, Hokmah; and Ipsissimus, Keter.[10]

Each rank was assigned two numbers signifying how far the person in the rank was from the spiritual world (the top of the Tree) and the physical world (the bottom of the Tree). For example, the Zelator is designated 1^0-10^0, one degree above the physical world and ten degrees below the world of total spirit. Adeptus Minor, located in Tifaret, is designated 5^0=6^0; five degrees above the totally physical, six degrees below the totally spiritual.[11]

The nature of the hierarchy, then, was that spirit was at the top and matter at the bottom.

In another marked departure from Jewish tradition, two paths were added at the bottom of the Tree, connecting Malkut to both Hod and Netsach. As discussed in the previous chapters, Jewish Kabbalah allows no path to Malkut except from Yesod. Traditionally, there are twenty-two paths connecting the sefirot. In Jewish Kabbalah, two paths, which are missing on the Qabalah glyph, go from Hokmah to Gevurah and from Binah to Hesed, conforming with the example of emanation given by Cordovero (see page 32). The differences in the path placements reflect differences between Kabbalah and Qabalah in the relationships among sefirot and in the intent of rituals. Qabalists did not seem particularly interested in opening additional channels of emanation to Malkut. Rather the reason for the addition of two paths at the bottom of the Tree apparently is to provide extra paths for Golden Dawn members to traverse in their climb. And since the paths at the top were not used for this purpose, two could easily be deleted there to still have the required twenty-two. Also, fewer paths at the top made the hierarchy at the highest levels more clear-cut and autocratic.

Absolute secrecy and obedience to those higher up the organizational hierarchy was required of Golden Dawn members. Each rank carried with it knowledge of a different secret password and handshake.

Upon becoming a member of the Golden Dawn, the neo-phyte pledged:

❀ to keep secret the order's name, the names of its members, its proceedings, and any other information about the order

❀ not to try to get a copy of any of the order's rituals or lectures without first getting permission from "the Praemonstrator of my Temple" who would properly label it with the "official label" of the Golden Dawn

❀ not to be hypnotized nor placed in any state so passive that the member might lose control of his or her thoughts, words, or actions (and thus reveal the order's secrets)

❀ not to use occult powers for evil purposes.

Despite the last pledge, if the member broke any of the pledges, he or she promised to undergo "the awful penalty of voluntarily submitting myself to a deadly and hostile current of will set in motion by the chiefs of the Order, by which I should fall slain and paralyzed without visible weapon as if slain by lightning flash."[12] In other words, although all members were pledged not to use occult powers for evil purposes, the chiefs were justified in unleashing "a deadly and hostile current of will" if members broke a pledge.

Foremost among the several types of Golden Dawn rituals were those marking the passages of the members as they climbed the Tree. These rituals included Wiccan-like actions and symbolism, such as:

❀ Circumambulation. Similar to Wiccan practice of "casting a circle," which, however, is usually accomplished with one person moving around the circle of participants. In the Golden Dawn practice the

entire group walked three times around the temple
in the "direction of the sun" representing the rising of spiritual light. Circumambulation began at
east, then went south, west, and north. The ritual
ended with a reverse direction "circumambulation,"
similar to the Wiccan opening of a circle at the end
of a ritual.

❀ The association of the four elements and four directions are the same (East, air; South, fire; West,
water; North, earth).

❀ Purification of participants with water, and
"consecration" with incense.

❀ Inscription of pentagrams and other symbols in the
air with swords and wands. The pentagram was understood to be a symbol of Malkut, bride of what
the qabalists called the Microprosopos[13] (referring
to Tifaret and/or the sefirot from Hesed to Yesod
and meaning literally small face; the equivalent to
the Lurianic short face).

The qabalists added Egyptian and other Goddess and God
symbolism. For example, members represented the goddesses
Isis, Nepthys, and Hathor in rituals. Isis was considered to be
in the sefirot Netsach, and Nepthys in Hod. In the ritual of
the twenty-eighth path, part of the Philosophus ritual, a priestess wearing the mask of Isis says:

"I am the rain of Heaven descending upon the Earth. . . I am
the plenteous yielder of the harvest. I am the cherisher of Life."

A priestess wearing the mask of Nepthys says: "I am the
dew, descending noiseless and silent, germinating the Earth. . .
bearing down the influence from above in the solemn darkness of Night."

A priestess wearing Hathor's mask says: "I am the Ruler of
the Mist and Cloud, wrapping the Earth as it were with a gar-

ment, floating and hovering between Earth and Heaven. I am the Giver of the Mist, the Veil of Autumn, the successor of the dew-clad Night."

Yet while allowing the presence of the female deities, the ritual is quick to assert the supremacy of the Father God: "For in the whole Universe shineth the Triad, over which the [Paternal] Monad ruleth. . . . For the Mind of the Father said that all things should be cut in three. . . Thus floweth forth the form of the Triad. . .not the first essence. . . ."

Similarly, in the Practicus ritual, a particularly lyrical passage describes the male and female divine:

"The Sun. . . is the centre of the triple world. The Sun is Fire and the dispenser of Fire. He is also the channel for the Higher Fire.

"And the Great Goddess bringeth forth the vast Sun and brilliant Moon, and the wide Air, and the Lunar Course and the Solar Pole. She collecteth it, receiving the melody of the Aether and of the Sun and of the Moon and whatever is contained in Air. Unwearied doth Nature rule over the Worlds and Works, so that the period of all things may be accomplished. And above the shoulders of the Great Goddess is Nature in Her vastness exalted."

Yet the same ritual affirms: ". . .all things are subservient through the Will of the Father of All."[14]

Here not only is male dominance affirmed, but also the Father has taken on the epithet associated with the Goddess (Mother of all).

A Goddess called Dadouches was also represented by one of the members during the rituals. Called "The Goddess of the Balance at the White Pillar," her name was also Thoum-aesh-neith, which appears to be an elaboration of the Goddess Neith.

The post of Hegemon, another Goddess figure represented by a member, was considered to have triple form and dual characteristics. The member representing Hegemon sat at the "symbolic gateway of occult sciences," and was considered the reconciler between dark and light.[15]

In addition to Pagan and specifically Egyptian and Greek symbolism, the Golden Dawn attached Christian symbolism to the Tree. The first three sefirot (Keter, Hokmah, Binah) were considered to represent the Christian trinity[16] despite the fact that the Christian trinity has no female equivalent of Binah. (Though some feminist theologians have proposed "The Holy Spirit" as the feminine part of the Christian trinity, this image is most like the more abstract nature of Keter, not the more concrete womblike image of Binah.) Further, the upper qabalistic trinity has no equivalent of the Christian Son.

That image is given to Tifaret. This is consistent with its Jewish kabbalistic meaning. The Golden Dawn further Christianized Tifaret by specifying that Tifaret was not only Adam but also Christ—more specifically the crucified Christ—referred to as "the second Adam." Qabalists also call this sefirah "Heaven" and consider it the "heart of the Sephirotic Tree." Golden Dawn's symbol of Tifaret is a red cross, and the interpretation of this sefirah is derived from the "rosy cross" theosophy of Rosicrucianism.

Christian angels and archangels were all given homes on the Tree. Ten of them were seen as inhabiting the world of Briah, one assigned to each sefirah, with the angel Metatron seen as "the commander," governing the visible world, including the stars and planets under the will of God. Angelic choirs were seen as dwelling the world of Yetsirah. The interpretation of these worlds is fairly close to the Lurianic interpretation, except that the world of Assiyah has become darker, more foreboding, and more closely identified with the material world. It was considered the "Abode of Darkness wherein dwell the grosser shells or spirits. . . energies or forces destructive to man, because they are further removed from the primordial source."[17]

The sefirah Malkut, located at the bottom of Assiyah, is described as the evil part of the Tree of Good and Evil and as the kingdom of the "shells." Malkut is related to the element earth, and as such is "the receptacle" of air, fire, and water. Because of her earthiness or closeness to the material plane, Malkut is considered to contain evil, which needs to be purged by fire and water.[18]

To Malkut were assigned several Christian personifications: the three "holy Women" (i.e., the Marys) at the foot of the cross; also just Mary, Mother of Jesus; and also Eve. The representation of Malkut as the three Marys could be seen as a reference to the triple Goddess. The symbolism, of Mary and Eve, however, contain more negative connotations.

For example: ". . . the Son should be crucified on the Cross of the infernal Rivers in Daath; yet to do this He must descend to the lowest first, even unto Malkuth and be born of Her."[19] The implication here is clearly that Malkut/Mary is "lowly," as is woman, but that in order to fulfill his mission, Christ had to lower himself to be born of woman.

And though Golden Dawn rituals at times referred to Eve as "Mother of all," and "the Great Goddess," she is seen as shirking in her duty to support the sefirotic pillars by "being tempted by the Tree of Knowledge," and thereby bringing about the Fall.[20] In earlier kabbalistic doctrine, Adam brought about the fall, or cosmic catastrophe, by mistaking Malkut for all of divinity. But in Qabalah, Eve/Goddess herself causes the catastrophe which becomes something that happens to Adam.[21] Though, in a way, this could be seen as a positive step, since it bolsters the importance of the divine female's responsibility and at least gives the female power enough to cause a cosmic catastrophe, the ultimate effect of this shift is stronger theological support for misogynist viewpoints.

The three pillars Goddess Eve was supposed to be supporting contain the sefirot and paths. There are three pillars or columns: middle, right, and left. The middle pillar mediates between the right and the left pillars. The right pillar is considered active and masculine, the left is considered passive and feminine. The right pillar is symbolic of Adam, the left, of Eve. They also represent the two cherubim guarding the Ark in the Temple: the male Metatron and the female Sandolphon. [22]

This oppositional stereotyping carried over into the Golden Dawn's ritual work. For example, the order's seven ritual officers, which represented "powers not persons" were considered either positive (active) and male or negative (passive) and female, "according to the god-form used." That is, if addressed or considered as a female deity, the "power" had a passive/negative connotation, if male, its connotation was active/positive.

The Golden Dawn offers a graphic description of the place of the serpent, as well as the status of female deity, in its depiction of the qabalistic Tree before and after the Fall.

Before the Fall, atop the Tree (specifically atop the middle pillar), in an enlarged sefirah bearing the wings of Isis, was none other than the crowned Goddess. A sunburst over her midsection (encompassing her womb), she stands atop a crescent moon labeled "Supernal Eden." The right and left pillars stop before reaching her sefirah. A nude, crowned and bearded male figure is below her on the center pillar (just below the sefirah related to Tifaret), supporting a crosspath with Hesed and Gevurah. The area at the height of the man's legs between the pillars is labeled "the knowledge of good." He stands atop a sefirah (Yesod) just above a crowned nude female figure who supports the right and left pillars from below. She stands atop a sefirah at the location of Malkut, which contains the eight-headed serpent. This area is labeled "The knowledge of evil," and emphasizes the Golden Dawn's location of evil in Malkut.

The depiction of the Tree after the Fall shows a large circle containing three sefirot represented by a crown (Keter), a crowned, bearded male head shown full face on the right (Hokmah), and a crowned female head (Binah) on his left, shown in profile, turned away from him.

The eight-headed serpent has broken free of its containment in the Malkut-like sefirah, running amok as far up as the location of Tifaret. A lightening bolt and Hebrew letters representing the Holy Name separate the serpent from the three upper sefirot. On the middle pillar, the head and shoulders of a crownless woman are shown touching the area from which the serpent has escaped. Above her, midst the snakes, is the head and shoulders of a crownless man.

The Golden Dawn explanation of the "before" depiction is that the three supernals (Keter, Hokmah, and Binah) were "summed up. . . in Aima Elohim, the Mother Supernal." This is the depiction in Revelations 12 of "a woman clothed with the sun, and the moon under her feet, and upon her head a crown of the twelve stars."[23] Those familiar with Goddess spirituality will recognize this vision of the Great Goddess. The Golden Dawn interpreted the crown with twelve stars as Keter. The man whose arms are outstretched to Gedulah [Hesed] and Gevurah is Adam and the woman in Malkut is Eve.

After the Fall, the union of the supernals is shattered; and in an explanation reminiscent of the Lurianic catastrophe, the lower sefirot are separated from the three upper supernals; and evil, symbolized by the serpents, is let loose on the Tree.

Yet the Golden Dawn has, perhaps unintentionally, given us a picture of "the Fall" as the fall—or the catastrophic cessation—of Goddess worship. For in the first depiction we see the Goddess as the sole divinity, understood to also contain the male god (or the masculine face of Goddess!). When she is recognized and honored, both man and woman are also crowned with honor, an honor which is connected to their sharing responsibility for the wholeness of divinity and for the well-being of creation. After "the Fall," which also can be seen here as the fragmentation of the Goddess, male and female can no longer be understood as full bodies—full people; they are depicted either as just heads or heads and shoulders. That is, without the wholeness of the Goddess, humans cannot be integrated spirit, intellect, and body; they are only "talking heads"—intellect only. Further, as shown at the top of the Tree, woman and man—even in the divine world—do not see each other fully, there is a rift between them.

A puzzling element is the Golden Dawn's persisting to use the Christian representation of the serpent as evil despite their recognition of the positive serpent symbolism.

For example, in the Philosophus Ritual, the initiate is led to the "Tablet of the Serpent of Brass in the East," and told that it is: "the Serpent, Nehushtan, which Moses made. . . it is the serpent of the Paths of the Tree. . . . and he twined it round the Middle Pillar of the Sephirot. . . because that is the reconciler between the Waters of Chesed. . . and hence it is said . . . that it is a sign of Christ, the Reconciler. . . he is also the Celestial Serpent of Wisdom, but the Serpent of Temptation is the Serpent of the Tree of Knowledge of Good and Evil and not that of the Tree of Life." Further, while the Serpent of Evil could rise no higher than Daath, in at least two other representations of a serpent, presumably the one of wisdom, it is shown winding around all sefirot up to and including Keter.[24]

So there seems to be a good serpent and a bad serpent. Could this be similar to the earlier kabbalistic doctrine of the Malkut/Shekinah having good and bad aspects?

Golden Dawn's attempted reconciliation of the opposing serpent symbolism does not seem adequate. Perhaps the confusion persists due to a lack of understanding of how the serpent came to be changed from a symbol of divinity, healing, and transformation connected with the Goddess to a symbol of evil, with the effect of demonizing both the Goddess and woman. This confusion is evident in the order's presentation of female and male divinity and especially in the demonization of Malkuth.

Perhaps this ambivalence or confusion was even welcomed by the order. For it no doubt added to the difficulty of understanding the order's concepts which, to its members, was a plus. Golden Dawn leaders were known to sometimes make things obscure on purpose to confuse noninitiates.[25] If initiates were also confused, they could always believe that as they progressed up the Tree, things would be made clearer to them during their studies or during the rituals, which progressively revealed the "secrets" of esoteric thought.

DEVELOPMENT OF QABALAH CONTINUES

The qabalist known to us as Dion Fortune joined the Golden Dawn in 1919, several years after its heyday and after the death of Mathers. Her "real" name was Violet Firth Evans. Like other members, upon initiation she adopted a Latin motto. Her Golden Dawn motto, Deus Non Fortune (God not Luck), became the basis of her pen name, with its meaning changed to include the Goddess Fortuna. She became dissatisfied with the Golden Dawn, mainly because of the dearth of metaphysical instruction available to her in the order.[26] She left the order, studied a great deal on her own, and founded in London the Fraternity (later known as Society) of Inner Light.

In her book *The Mystical Qabalah*, first published in England in 1935, she revealed some of the Golden Dawn material and added her own interpretations. The philosophy of Qabalah she set forth, particularly the interpretations of the sefirot, are the most widely accepted by today's qabalists, including those practicing in many metaphysical, New Age, and Wiccan groups.

Fortune describes three planes of "unmanifestation" and four planes of manifestation. The three planes of unmanifestation (also called "negative existence" or the three Veils) are an adaptation of the kabbalistic addition of a three-part Ein Sof; here the division is called Ein (negativity), Ein Soph (the limitless), and Ein Soph Aur (limitless light). Keter is emanated from the Ein Soph Aur.

The four planes of manifestation are Atzilut, Briah, Yetsirah, and Assiyah. The level of Atzilut, Fortune explains, contains only Keter, the "vast countenance" (an alternative translation of the Lurianic "long-faced one"). It is the world of emanation, which she also calls the archetypal world. It corresponds to the element of fire and the Tarot suite of wands. The second level, that of Briah, which contains Hokmah and Binah, is called the creative world, and is that which is manifested from the "vast countenance." It corresponds to the element of water and the Tarot the suit of cups. Yetsirah is composed of the six sefirot from Hesed to Yesod, which she calls the "lesser countenance" (an alternative translation of the Lurianic term for these sefirot); it is the formative world. It corresponds to the element air, and the Tarot suit of swords. Assiyah has only one sefirah, Malkuth, the material world. It corresponds to the element earth and to the Tarot suit of Pentacles. Although Fortune says (in an interpretation similar to pre-Lurianic Kabbalah) that all ten sefirot can be considered to appear in each world, she maintains that Atzilut is the "natural sphere" of the sefirot. In Atzilut, she says, God works directly; in Briah, through archangels; in Yetsirah, through angelic orders; and in Assiyah, through planets, elements, and signs of the zodiac.[27]

Like kabbalists beginning with Cordovero, Fortune sees the sefirotic tree as containing polarities labeled masculine and feminine which need to be moderated and balanced. Yet

Fortune's interpretation seems to even further polarize the genders. As before, the sefirot appear on three pillars. The left pillar (as we look at it), called "Severity," is feminine. It is also considered negative and passive. Its sefirot are Binah, Gevurah/Din, and Hod. The right pillar, called "Mercy" is masculine, positive, and active. Its sefirot are Hokmah, Hesed/Gedullah, and Netsach. The middle pillar, called "Mildness" mediates between the two pillars and contains Keter, the "invisible sefirot" Da'at, Tifaret, Yesod, and Malkut. Keter and Malkut do not mediate, however. Keter emanates and Malkut receives (through the other sefirot) all emanations. Da'at mediates Hokmah and Binah; Tifaret, Hesed and Gevurah; and Yesod, Netsach and Hod.

This stereotyping of feminine as negative and passive and masculine as the positive and active is detrimental to women and inaccurate. The description of the sefirot deepens this bias, despite Fortune's continued attempts to affirm the feminine/female divine. (The qabalistic correspondences for the ten sefirot can be seen beginning on page 100.)

Fortune describes Keter as having no form; as "pure being" but not a person, a unity. She says that during her metaphysical work, she touched the "fringe" of Keter and it appeared as a "blinding white light, in which all thought went completely blank." But, she says, Keter can also be understood as the darkness of interstellar space. Keter is "of our cosmos but not in it," she says; it belongs to another dimension.

She says that Keter is forever in a state of becoming (presaging Existential philosophy of the mid-twentieth century) and prefers translating its godname, Eheyeh "I will be," rather than the traditional, "I am."

However, Fortune presents Keter's representative image as male: an ancient bearded king straight out of Lurianic Kabbalah and calls him by the name Macroprosopos, the

qabalistic term for the Lurianic "long-faced one." She com-
pares Keter to the "Father of the gods," "the Sky God."[28]

In matching the Christian trinity to the sefirot, she says
that Keter is the "sphere of three in one. . . the undivided unity";
Tifaret is the sphere of the Redeemer or Son; and Yesod is the
Sphere of the Holy Spirit.[29] However, we note that the first
person of the Christian trinity (here given as Keter) is the Father.

Fortune says that her assignment of the Christian trinity
to three of the center sefirot fits better than the Golden Dawn's
assignment of the Son to Hokmah and the Holy Spirit to Binah.
She maintains that the Golden Dawn assignment produces
many discrepancies in correspondences and symbolism. However, we will see that neither the Golden Dawn's nor Fortune's
Christian trinity attributions really "fit" and that they both dis-
tort the original intent.

The paired sefirot, Fortune says, need to be understood in
relation to each other, for they are polarities. Hokmah, the
Supernal Father, is unorganized force, an "outflowing of bound-
less energy. It is "The Great Stimulator of the Universe."

"The Father," she says, "is the giver of life; but the Mother
is the giver of death because her womb is the gate of ingress to
matter. . ." Here, reflecting the social and religious beliefs of
her time, Fortune couples disdain for matter with disdain for
the physical womb—and by extension, women.

Because Binah opposes Hokmah's dynamic impulses, she is
seen as the "enemy of God, the evil one." Fortune says, however,
that Qabalah teaches a "wiser doctrine: that all sefirot are holy."[30]

Though we certainly agree with this wiser doctrine, we also
object to the female/feminine being portrayed as the location
of evil—or of being in opposition to "God."

In the Golden Dawn tradition, Fortune presents these polarities: Hokmah=Positive=Maleness; Binah= Negative=Femaleness.

She does point out, however, that according to the *Sefir Yetsirah*, Binah is the "sanctifying intelligence." She says that the Virgin Mary is associated with Binah (although, as mentioned, the Golden Dawn associated her with Malkut).

Hokmah, Fortune says, "supplies the energy, and Binah supplies the machine."[31] Thus she continues the idea of the Supernal Mother as the empty vessel, dependent on the Father for energy.

Da'at (Knowledge) is envisioned as an "invisible sefirah." This departs from Cordovero's concept of Da'at as the sefirot through which we can "know" Keter and therefore synonymous with it. In the qabalistic interpretation, Da'at is included in an area called the Abyss which, in an interpretation similar to Luria's, was formed during the catastrophic Fall.

Again, as in Lurianic doctrine, the next six sefirot combine into the "lesser countenance," which the qabalists call Microprosopos, and which they also acknowledge as the Adam Kadmon or the King. The next two sefirot, Hesed (also called Gedullah) and Gevurah (also called Din) are opposites that must work together. They are both imaged as kings: Hesed as a crowned and enthroned king; Gevurah as a warrior king in his chariot. And although both images are male, it is interesting to note that the beneficent king makes his home on the masculine pillar and the violent king on the feminine pillar. This is consistent with the assignment of negative, evil forces to the sefirot on the feminine pillar (and to Malkut). Hesed (on masculine pillar) builds things up, while Gevurah (on the feminine pillar), breaks things down. Hesed is associated with idealism, Gevurah with realism. Hesed does the creative work of the world, formulating archetypal and abstract ideas. He is the home of "The Masters," highly evolved beings who are free of the wheel of birth and death. Gevurah, on the left side, is home of the "Dark Masters."

Tifaret aids in balancing the forces of Hesed and Gevurah, but even more than that, in Qabalah, Tifaret is the center of equilibrium of the whole Tree. It is the center of the six sefirot composing the Adam Kadmon. It is, Fortune says, Keter on a "lower arc." It should never be considered an isolated factor, but "as a link. . . a center of transition or transmutation. . . between planes of force and planes of form." When the adept is ascending the Tree, Tifaret represents seership, which is attained after working through the next lower three sefirot: Netsach, the location of nature forces; Hod, the place of ceremonial magic and occult knowledge; and Yesod, the site of psychic work that involves the interpretation of symbolism. Tifaret is the place of higher consciousness which "is never psychic, but always intuitive, containing no sensory imagery."

Tifaret is the "place of incarnation" and the location of the Redeemer who strives to unite his Kingdom (Malkut) with the Supernals "across the gulf made by the Fall." In Christianity, Fortune says, it is the Christ center and all references to "the Son" refer to Tifaret. It is also the center of Dionysis, Osiris, and all other "givers of illumination" through ecstasy. (She locates the focus of what she calls pantheistic Greek and Egyptian religions in Yesod, and what she calls the metaphysical faiths such as Buddhism and Confucianism in Keter.) And in a statement with which we take exception, she says that the Son redeems "pantheistic nature worship from debasement."[32] Nature religions, in our view, need no redemption; they are not debased.

Netsach and Hod are the sefirot of the god/desses, other than those located in Tifaret. Fortune discusses what she feels is the appropriate response to the question: "Do you believe in the gods?" by saying that if the person venturing into occult science answers "yes," the person will wander "in the planes of illusion, for the gods are not real persons, as we understand personality." But if the person answers "no," the person will be "turned back at the gate, for the gods are not illusions." She reconciles this seeming paradox by telling us that the "gods are the creations of the created." They are emanations of the group-mind, not emanations of "Eheieh, the One and Eternal." Yet once these forms have been created, they "become channels of the specialized forces they were designed to represent."

In other words, a god or goddess, then, begins as a symbolic image, but spiritual "forces" then attach themselves to the image, ensouling it and making it real and active. Therefore, Fortune says, those in occult science not only believe in the god/desses, "they adore them." Further, she says that when working on the astral plane, the forms on that plane appear to the human consciousness as "ethereal forms of a distinctly human type. . . these forms of life, left to their own devices, achieve incarnation in natural phenomena." But they can sometimes be persuaded to make use of the forms created by the group-mind, one of the goals of magic.

These "life-forms" are located in Netsach, but they are acted upon through "magical operations" in Hod. Therefore, she says, the two sefirot are not clear-cut in their divisions.

Nevertheless, she offers these polarized attributes: Netsach, located on the male pillar, is the sphere of Venus, pictured as a beautiful naked women, where all kinds of love—not just sexual love—are located. Also located here are instincts, emotions, and the group-mind. Hod, on the female pillar, is the sphere of Mercury (also known as Hermes and Thoth). Located here are intellect, concrete (or the beginnings of the human) mind, scientific thinking, and magical workings.

She says, "it is by means of dance and sound and color that the Netsach angels are contacted and evoked."[33]

The qabalistic view of Netsach and Hod and, as we will see, Yesod, is perhaps the area in which it differs most from the

Jewish kabbalistic interpretations. In Jewish Kabbalah, the most common representation of Hod and Netsach is as the testicles of the Adam Kadmon, or, as two of the sefirot that aid the re-unification of God and the Shekinah. But the main concern of qabalists is not reunification, apparently because redemption is being facilitated by Christ in Tifaret. Further, qabalists needed a place to locate the pantheons of other religions and magical workings.

The most curious part of qabalistic Netsach-Hod is the location of female traits and representations on the male pillar and vice versa. This seeming confusion in sexual imagery continues in the next sefirot, Yesod, which in Jewish Kabbalah, represents the phallus.

Fortune agrees that the two sets of symbols qabalists attribute to Yesod are incongruous. The first set includes the term "foundation of the universe," which, as we learned, is a hyperbolic euphemism for the penis, the trait strength, and a picture of a naked man. The second set includes the feminine symbolism of the Moon and fluidity. To further muddy the waters, Fortune says that Yesod comes "under the presidency" of the Goddess Diana, and assigns the Moon a positive connotation and Earth (assigned to Malkut) a negative one.

Fortune explains the incongruity of male and female symbolism by referring to a text from *Sefir Yetsirah* saying that Yesod purifies and organizes the emanations. However, in my view, this text refers to Yesod's function as a phallus, through which the emanations (in this case, seminal fluid) are "organized" as they flow from the "testicles" of Netsach and Hod. That emanations might be purified in Yesod, does not explain why contradictory imagery should be located there. The explanation lies rather, I believe, in the departures qabalists made philosophically from Jewish ideology and in their need to locate all symbolism (in this case, a place was needed for the Moon) somewhere on the Tree. The distortions that occur in the qabalistic assignment of attributes to Hod, Netsach, and Yod are at least equal to those Fortune criticized in the Golden Dawn assignment of the Christian trinity to the first three sefirot.

Malkut, in its qabalistic presentation, is divided into four quarters, to which are assigned the four elements and which are represented by four colors. The citrine (water) quarter is positioned towards Yesod; the olive (air), towards Netsach; the russet (fire) towards Hod; and black (earth), towards "the Qliphoth," the unbalanced or destructive aspects of the sefirot, located at the bottom of the cube, the part closest to earth, to materiality.

Yesod represents a "coherence of parts" and "ensouls Malkuth." It is the vehicle of life and electrical activity, containing the procreative organs. Malkut manifests or materializes what is formed in Yesod. Malkut is inanimate without Yesod. Malkut's body correspondence is the anus.[34]

Again, despite the confusion of correspondences, the message is that Yesod (male) has the positive, active, creative traits, whereas Malkut (female) is an empty vessel until filled by Yesod; she is passive, tarnished, the location of the unsavory, even evil aspects of being.

Yet Fortune points out that "every magical operation must come through to Malkuth. . . for only in Malkuth is the force finally locked home into form. Therefore, all magical work is better carried out in the form of a ritual performed on the physical plane. . . than simply as a form of meditation." Further, she says that all divination is worked in Malkut. She also sees Malkut and Keter as opposites, saying that "the Great Mother, which is Malkuth, polarizes with the All-Father, which is Keter."[35]

Again, there is confusion about whether Keter is truly ungendered as claimed. Certainly here we have male gender attributed to Keter in a way that seems to go beyond previous kabbalistic characterizations of Keter as what Wolfson calls a male androgyne and establishes Keter as only male. In any case, we contend that "balances" or even better "complements" are better concepts for male and female relationships than "polarities."

QABALAH AND KABBALAH

In a way, Qabalah can be seen as an extension of Lurianic doctrine, just as Luria's teachings were permutations of kabbalistic thought preceding him. The additions of Egyptian, Greek, and other traditions can be considered within kabbalistic tradition, which itself combines with Jewish beliefs, concepts borrowed from Greek, Gnostic, and other Middle Eastern traditions.

Yet when we compare the concepts of Jewish Kabbalah and the Qabalah of the Western esoteric tradition, the following important differences are apparent:

- ❀ In Qabalah, the main work of humans is no longer the reunification of the female and male parts of divinity. Rather, Qabalah views this as occurring through the moderation by the center pillar of the polarities of the right and left pillars.
- ❀ There have been significant changes in the meaning and symbolism of all sefirot, the most extreme changes being in Hesed through Yesod.
- ❀ The concepts of the separation of spirit from matter, and the depiction of spirit as good and matter as evil, have been strengthened. Malkut is understood as being even more separated from the rest of the sefirot and is the location of unbalanced forces (previously located by the Zohar in Gevurah).
- ❀ Tifaret is seen as the Christ-center, a concept of course unknown in Jewish Kabbalah. Tifaret/Christ

is seen as having the task of uniting the three supernals (Keter, Hokmah, and Binah) with Malkut, now seen as "his Kingdom." The goal of this activity is to repair the damage caused by "the Fall."

❀ The concept of sacred sex as a way to reunify God and the Shekinah appears to be absent. In fact, if the way Golden Dawn leaders lived can be taken to be outcomes of their spiritual beliefs, sex has become "dirty" and chastity a virtue, the opposite of Jewish kabbalistic beliefs.

For example, Golden Dawn leaders MacGregor and Moina Mathers had a sexless marriage, supposedly because the "chiefs" (unnamed authorities from whom MacGregor supposedly took his orders) forbade MacGregor to have sex so that he could use that energy for spiritual work. Yeats was involved in a sexless "spiritual marriage" or union (they were never legally married) with Maude Gonne, whom he nevertheless desired physically. As was common in the Victorian times, Yeats had put Gonne on a pedestal, so that when, after several years of their relationship, she revealed to him her previous sexual activity with another man, the thought disgusted Yeats. From time to time, however, he would broach the possibility of having sex with Gonne; she responded that as a result of her spiritual work (and possibly her work for Irish Catholic Ireland) she was no longer interested in sex. Though Yeats masturbated through the years of this "union," he claimed that each instance of solo sex made him physically ill.[36]

Fortune departs from separation of sex and spirit somewhat, saying, in what may be a comment aimed at these earlier Golden Dawn members: ". . . the Mysteries do not teach asceticism or celibacy as a requirement or achievement, because they do not regard spirit and matter as unreconcilable. . . but rather as different levels of the same thing." Yet since sex is "one aspect of . . . polarity. . . that runs through all of creation," she condemns homosexuality as "perverted and pathological." She says that it only occurs because the "polarity of the sexes" is not correctly understood.[37]

As seen from the standpoint of today's Goddess spirituality, Fortune's (and the Golden Dawn's) view of Qabalah presents us with ambivalent or conflicting ideas. Their impulse certainly was to include the feminine/female in divinity. But emerging from the Victorian era, and still working under a patriarchal system, some basic assumptions kept them from arriving at a consistent and liberating spirituality.

For example, in her view of nature, Fortune seems to want to break away from the Golden Dawn outlook equating nature with dirtiness or even evil. She says, "the person who is cut off from his instincts, which are his roots in Mother Earth . . . cannot be an open channel through which power can be brought down. . ." On the other hand, the context in which she says this is in emphasizing the importance of what she calls "phallicism," that is the sexual element in magic and mysticism. This, then, defines all sexuality as focused on the male, which is well within the Jewish kabbalistic tradition. Extending the biological misconception to spiritual matters, Fortune says, "It is the male force that implants the fecundating spark in the passive ovum on all planes and transforms its inert latency into the active upbuilding of growth and evolution."[38]

As we have seen, Fortune still incorporates the idea that Malkut is the location of unsavory forces. But her definition of the Qliphoth or "shells" (or what are referred to as the "evil" sefirot) seems to modify the Golden Dawn definition. She defines the Qliphoth as the negative, unbalanced or destructive aspect of the sefirot which are nonetheless a necessary and integral part of the divine whole. Therefore, the "contending forces" should not be classified as "good" and "evil." She rejects this dualism, calling it heresy. Rather, she says, we should think in terms of reaching an equilibrium. She rejects the conflict between "light and darkness, spirit and matter" that results in "the triumph of the god and the total . . . elimination of all opposing influences." She says, "We cannot deal with evil by cutting it off and destroying it, but only by absorbing it and harmonizing it."[39]

Although rejecting these dualisms, Fortune continues to accept the equation good=light=spirit; evil=dark=matter. She does see as the goal equilibrium rather than victory (or, we might today call it up/down or one-upsmanship), but she nevertheless retains the stereotypes.

This is typical of the qabalistic view. It is open to many different paths, it strives to incorporate the female/feminine divine (as well as the male); yet it has not gotten rid of sexist patriarchal stereotypes. These stereotypes assign negative/passive qualities to the female and positive/active qualities to the male; they separate matter from spirit, tingeing matter with an evil quality—a tinge that extends to the female/feminine, which is equated with matter.

Though contemporary authors have tried to update Qabalah, sometimes by relating it to Wiccan concepts, Jungian psychology, or even feminist anthropological theory, this work is incomplete because it continues to accept Kabbalah/Qabalah's underlying patriarchal polarities, hierarchies, and stereotypes. For, as we have come to understand with the traditional Christian concept of Mary as a passive, empty vessel, it does little good to incorporate the concept of the female/feminine in divinity, if that concept reinforces the stereotype of women as tinged by evil (which must be kept under control), and passive—an empty vessel waiting to be filled by male "emanations."

EMBELLISHING THE TREE

Qabalistic Correspondences

In addition to these correspondences, the following are also assigned to each sefirot: an archangel and an order of angels, animals, plants, precious stones and metals, drugs, perfumes and incense, magical tools, and Tarot cards.

The Tarot correspondences begin with the aces of each suit (wands, cups, swords, pentacles) in Keter, the twos in Hokmah and so on to the tens in Malkut; the kings are in Hokmah, the queens in Binah, knights in Tifaret, and pages (or princesses) in Malkut; to the paths are assigned the twenty-two major arcana cards.[40]

Keter (Crown)

Image: Right-side profile of ancient bearded king
Titles: Concealed of the Concealed, Ancient of Ancients, The Primordial Point, White Head, Macroprosopos (vast countenance), Lux Occulta, Lux Interna, Hebrew letter He (of Tetragrammaton—YHVH)
Godname: Eheieh (I am that I am)
Universe correspondence: First swirlings, outer space
Spiritual experience: Union with God
Virtue: Attainment
Vice: (None)
Human correspondence: Cranium, right side of face
Symbol: Point within a circle
Colors: Azilut—brilliance
　　　　　Briah and Yetsirah—white brilliance
　　　　　Assiyah—white, flecked with gold

Hokmah(Wisdom)

Image: Bearded male figure
Titles: Abba,the Supernal Father, Straight Line, Tetragrammaton (YHWH), Hebrew letter Yod (of Tetragrammaton)
Godname: Jehovah
Universe correspondence: Zodiac
Spiritual experience: Face-to-face vision of God
Virtue: Devotion
Vice: (None)
Human correspondence: Left side of face
Symbols: Phallus, tower, straight line
Colors: Azilut—soft blue
> Briah—gray
> Yetsirah—pearl gray with iridescence
> Assiyah—white flecked with red, blue, and yellow

Binah (Understanding)

Image: Mature woman
Titles: Ama, the dark sterile mother and Aima, the bright fertile mother; Supernal(or Superior) Mother; the Throne; Marah, the sea; Mother of All Living; the Womb
Godname: Jehovah Elohim
Universe correspondence: Saturn
Spiritual experience: Vision of sorrow
Virtue: Silence
Vice: Jealousy, greed
Human correspondence: Right side of face
Symbols: Yoni, cup or chalice, two-dimensional plane
Colors: Azilut—crimson
> Briah—black
> Yetsirah—dark brown
> Assiah—gray flecked with pink

Hesed/Gedullah (Mercy)

Image: Crowned and enthroned king
Titles: Love, Majesty, Loving Father, Protector, Lawgiver
Godname: El
Universe correspondence: Jupiter
Spiritual experience: Vision of love
Virtue: Obedience
Vices: Bigotry, hypocrisy, gluttony, tyranny
Human correspondence: Left arm
Symbols: Pyramid, equal-armed cross, orb, wand, scepter, tetrahedron, three-dimensional solid, pyramid
Colors: Atzilut—deep violet
        Briah—blue
        Yetsirah—deep purple
        Assiyah—deep azure, flecked with yellow

Gevurah/Din (Valor, Justice)

Image: Warrior in his chariot
Titles: Strength, Severity, Fear, Destroyer, Warrior
Godname: Elohim Gevor (God/desses of Valor)
Universe correspondence: Mars
Spiritual experience: Vision of power
Virtue: Energy, courage
Vice: Cruelty, destruction
Human correspondence: Right arm
Symbols: Sword, spear, chain, five-petaled rose, pentagon
Colors: Azilut—orange
        Briah—scarlet red
        Yetsirah—bright scarlet
        Assiyah—red flecked with black

Tifaret (Beauty)

Images: King, child, sacrificed god
Titles: Microprosopus (lesser countenance), Adam, the Son, the King
Godname: Tetragrammaton Aloah Va Daath (YHWH of Highest Knowledge or Ascended Knowledge)
Universe correspondence: The Sun
Spiritual experience: Vision of harmony, mysteries of Crucifixion
Virtue: Devotion to great mystical work
Vice: Pride
Human correspondence: Breast or solar plexus
Symbols: Rosy Cross, cube
Colors: Atzilut—rose-pink
   Briah—yellow
   Yetsirah—salmon-pink
   Assiyah—amber

Netsach (Victory)

Image: A beautiful naked woman
Title: Firmness
Godname: Jehovah Sabaot (Lord of Hosts)
Universe correspondence: Venus
Spiritual experience: Vision of beauty triumphant
Virtue: Unselfishness
Vice: Promiscuity, lust
Human correspondence: Loins, hips, and legs
Symbols: Lamp, rose
Colors: Azilut—amber
   Briah—emerald
   Yetsirah—bright chartreuse
   Assiyah—olive, flecked with gold

Hod (Glory)

Image: Hermaphrodite
Godname: Elohim Sabaot (God/desses of Hosts)
Universe correspondence: Mercury
Spiritual experience: Vision of splendor
Virtue: Truthfulness
Vice: Lying, dishonesty
Human correspondence: Loins and legs
Symbols: Names, apron, caduceus
Colors: Atzilut—violet-purple
      Briah—orange
      Yetzirah—russet
      Assiyah—yellowish black, flecked with white

Yesod (Foundation)

Image: Strong and beautiful naked man
Godname: Shaddai El Chai (Almighty Living God—literally, breasted God of life)
Universe correspondence: Moon
Spiritual experience: Vision of universe's machinery
Virtue: Independence
Vice: Idleness
Human correspondence: Sex organs
Symbol: Sandals
Colors: Atzilut—indigo
      Briah—violet
      Yetzirah—very dark purple
      Assiyah—citrine, flecked with azure

Malkut (Kingdom)

Image: A young woman, crowned and enthroned

Titles: The Gate, the Inferior Mother, the Queen, the Sabbath Bride, the Virgin

Godname: Adonai Malekh or Adonai ha Aretz (Lord of the Earth)

Universe correspondence: Earth

Spiritual Experience: Vision of the holy guardian angel

Virtue: Discernment

Vice: Greed, inertia

Human correspondence: Feet, anus

Symbols: Equal armed cross, circle, triangle

Colors: Azilut—yellow
> Briah—citrine, olive, russet, and black
> Yetsirah—citrine, olive, russet and black flecked with gold
> Assiyah—black, rayed with yellow

COMMENTS

TITLES

The assignment of the Hebrew letter "He" to Keter is curious since in Kabbalah it refers to the female part of the divine name, transliterated YHWH. Perhaps this is an unconscious reference to the previous name of Keter, the feminine Ru'ah?

The dual titles of Binah, Ama and Aima, are different transliterations of the same Hebrew word meaning mother. In giving these transliterations different meanings the qabalists continue the earlier kabbalistic view of the female part of divinity as having good and evil (symbolized by light and dark) sides.

GODNAMES

All Godnames on the "feminine" pillar end with the "im" plural Hebrew ending on a male noun, which can be taken to mean that the godname is masculine and feminine plural. Godnames on the "male" pillar are masculine singular.

VIRTUES AND VICES

As we descend the Tree, vices are not assigned to the sefirot until we reach the first female sefirah, Binah. Further, her virtue is silence, reminiscent of the biblical advice that women "learn in silence and with all subjection" (I Timothy 2:11-13). Fortune's explanation of the virtues and vices is that they are qualities necessary for a person to be initiated into that grade. The vice is the form taken by any unbalanced force in that sefirah. She says there are no vices in Keter and Hokmah because "formation" didn't occur until Binah.[41] So, in addition to the sexist assumption that formation and vice occur simultaneously in the first feminine sefirah, this explanation reinforces the separation between spirit and form (or matter).

HUMAN CORRESPONDENCES

The human correspondences are considered subjective and therefore a mirror image of the usual way of looking at the Tree.[42]

COLORS

It is interesting to compare these color correspondences with Cordovero's (see page 71). While the colors of Hokmah, Tifaret, and Gevurah are similar, there are significant departures in the colors of the other sefirot. For example, Keter has lost its blackness and now, apparently male, is seen only as brilliant. Binah is no longer green (connected to Earth and to growth) its colors now reflecting tarnishing by Binah's association with the earthly Malkut.

Chapter 5
Re-Visioning Kabbalah

On the desolate ruins wrought by heresy, the sublime knowledge of God will build her temple. Utter heresy arises to purify the air of the wicked, insolent filth of thinking about the essence of divinity. . . . What appeared to be heresy, now purified, is restored to perfect faith.
—Abraham Isaac Kook, twentieth-century kabbalist

We are digging up fragments rather than studying a coherent system; for the system, though coherent in its heyday, was broken and scattered and defaced by the persecutions of twenty centuries.
—Dion Fortune, twentieth-century qabalist

↶ FOR THOSE WHO SEEK to explore mystical or metaphysical paths consistent with Goddess spirituality, the underlying assumptions of Kabbalah/Qabalah may be discouraging.

These assumptions include:

❀ deity as male, or as a male androgyne with a feminine aspect, rather than deity as female, divine in her own right

❀ stereotypes of the female as receptive, passive, instinctual, and negative; and the male as creative, active, intellectual, and positive

❀ male and female as opposite polarities, rather than complements

❀ matter and spirit as separate and opposite; the female part of divinity located closest to matter and therefore incorporating evil

❀ separation of matter and spirit blamed on the female aspect of divinity and by extension on the carnality or evil inherent in women

❀ divinity described as hierarchy.

In addition, the overwhelmingly heterosexual biases of these systems seem to exclude homosexuals and bisexuals, many of whom find acceptance and blessing in Goddess spirituality.

But rather than abandon Kabbalah/Qabalah, what I believe is necessary is a re-visioning of the system, a purification which leads us back to its true roots: beginning with the Word. Or, to be more precise, the words.

As we have seen, the roots of the Tree are deep, going back to the beginning of human memory. The original concept has undergone enormous changes; to trace these changes is to trace the emergence and ultimate dominance of patriarchy. In examining these changes, we have identified many reversals of original intent. In language, the most obviously stunning and seemingly inexplicable is the sex-change of Hokmah.

This reversal is our first hint of other language changes. And it is through language, through words—through the titles given to the sefirot—that I believe we understand the true nature of the original intent of what we have received.

Let us begin, then, to look at Kabbalah in terms of the genders of the nouns given to each sefirah.

For example, as previously mentioned, the Hebrew Hokmah, a feminine-gendered noun, is translated Wisdom (equivalent to the Greek Sophia) and in biblical passages given female gender, in both the original language and English translation. In Kabbalah, however, Hokmah, while still translated as Wisdom, is called the "Supernal Father."

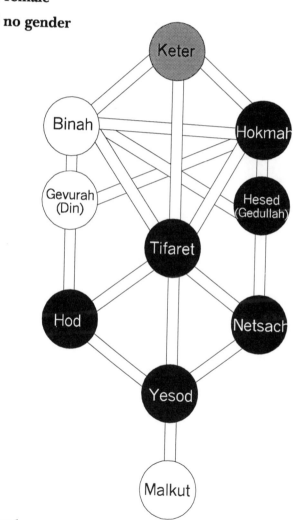

JEWISH KABBALAH
Traditional Sefirot Gender

- ● male
- ○ female
- ◐ no gender

Keter

Binah

Hokmah

Gevurah (Din)

Hesed (Gedullah)

Tifaret

Hod

Netsach

Yesod

Malkut

FIGURE 1

Qabalah
Sefirot Gender

● **male**
○ **female**

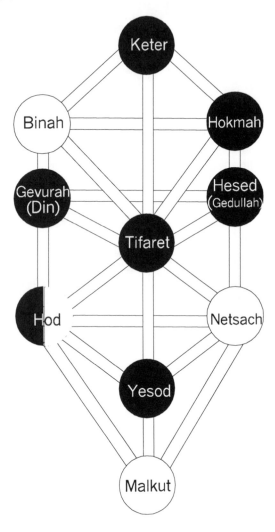

FIGURE 2

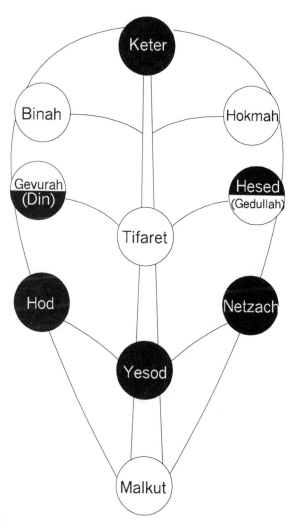

REVISIONED KABBALAH
By Sefirot Noun Genders

● male
○ female

Keter

Binah

Hokmah

Gevurah (Din)

Hesed (Gedullah)

Tifaret

Hod

Netzach

Yesod

Malkut

FIGURE 3

How can Hokmah be represented as male? There does not seem to be any satisfactory explanation in books or other writings. We have also learned that the name of the first sefirah was changed in early Kabbalah from the feminine Ru'ah (spirit) to the masculine Keter (Crown). In the light of these changes, what about the gender of the other sefirot? What else has been changed—reversed? And, ultimately, what was the original?

Figures 1 and 2 show the Trees of Kabbalah and Qabalah as traditionally represented, with sefirot shaded according to traditional gender. The first sefirah, Keter, according to kabbalistic tradition is the first point of emanation of divine light. It is supposedly genderless, but evolved masculine imagery by the time Qabalah evolved and has been imaged as a king with a long beard. Keter is emanated from an area atop the Tree, usually called in Kabbalah the Ein Sof, but especially in Qabalah composed of Ein (nothingness), Ein Sof (the infinite), and Ein Soph Aur (infinite light). In both Kabbalah and Qabalah, this area above Keter is considered the "root" from which the Tree grows downward.

After the second sefirah, Hokmah (Wisdom), the "Supernal Father," comes the third sefirah, Binah (Understanding), the "Supernal Mother." In Qabalah, Binah is seen as a dual Goddess, having both dark and bright aspects. In the Jewish tradition, she is seen as both "Virgin" and "Warrior,"[1] (the warrior image being Kali-like).

In Lurianic Kabbalah and Qabalah, the six sefirot following (or flowing from) Binah form the Adam Kadmon, the primordial man who serves as a link between the Ein Sof whose light he emanates to the "worlds" below.

The Western esoteric tradition is more specific than Jewish Kabbalah about the exact nature of the other sefirot. Their names in both systems, however, are (with some small variations) the same.

The fourth sefirah has two alternative names: Hesed, translated love, charity, or mercy, and Gedullah, translated greatness. The image, particularly in Qabalah, is an enthroned beneficent king. The fifth sefirah, which in seen as being in polarity with Hesed-Gedullah, is usually called Gevurah, usually translated as strength or valor, but also meaning hero or heroine. This sefirah is also called Din, judgment. Its image in Qabalah, is a warrior-king in his chariot. In Kabbalah, it usually has negative feminine attributes.

The sixth sefirah is Tifaret, translated beauty, splendor, or glory. In Jewish Kabbalah, the specific representation of this sefirah varies, sometimes called the King, or a biblical hero, but always male. It is the Adam Kadmon, which also extends to other sefirot. In Qabalah, the symbol can be the center of the Adam Kadmon, a king, a son, or a healing and/or sacrificed god, including Jesus Christ. It is considered the center or heart of the Tree.

The seventh sefirah, whose Hebrew name is Netsach, translated lasting endurance or victory, is understood in Kabbalah to represent one testicle of the Adam Kadmon. In Qabalah, it is characterized as a beautiful naked woman, reminiscent of the Goddess Venus.

The eighth sefirah, Hod, translated majesty, glory, or splendor, is understood in Kabbalah to be the Adam Kadmon's other testicle. In Qabalah it is imaged as a hermaphrodite.

The ninth, Yesod, translated foundation or basis, is understood in Kabbalah to be Adam Kadmon's penis. It is imaged in Qabalah as a strong, young, and attractive naked man, yet also symbolized by the Moon and other feminine imagery. Although also identifying this sefirah as male and phallic, Qabalah and some forms of Kabbalah locate both male and female genitals in Yesod.[2] This emphasizes the male-centered nature of sexual activity.

The tenth sefirah is Malkut, usually translated kingdom and represented in both Kabbalah and Qabalah as a Mother Earth figure. In Jewish Kabbalah, this sefirah is sometimes also called Atarah, translated diadem.

Looking at the sefirot according to their traditionally gendered images, in Kabbalah, one (Keter) is ungendered, with a decidedly masculine bent. In Qabalah, one (Hod) is a hermaphrodite. In both Kabbalah (diagram 1) and Qabalah (diagram 2), we see that of the ten sefirot, twice as many are male (six) as are female (three). Not exactly a balanced representation in systems that claim as goals balance between male and female and reunion of the female and male aspects of divinity.

But another picture entirely emerges when we look at the sefirot in terms of their Hebrew names.

Nouns have gender in many languages. In the context of everyday speech, few of us would make anything significant out of, for example, the word for "table" being feminine in Spanish. However, because Hebrew is so heavily gendered, as has been pointed out by scholars such as Judith Plaskow and Raphael Patai, it is impossible to approach Hebrew—particularly in its religious writings—without being aware of and taking seriously the gender of the words.[3] Further, Kabbalah itself defines the divine creative process as linguistic.[4] And because gendered images have been attached to the various sefirot we cannot help but ask: is the image attached to a particular sefirah consistent with its noun gender? And if not, why not?

Diagram 3 shows the sefirot as defined by the gender of their Hebrew nouns. It is startling, not only in its difference from the traditional symbolism, but in the sense that the pattern makes.

The first sefirah, Keter, is a masculine noun.[5] The second and third, Hokmah and Binah, are both feminine.

The fourth and fifth, which have two names each, can be seen as both female and male: The fourth sefirah's names are Hesed (masculine) and Gedullah (feminine); the fifth's are Gevurah, a noun with a feminine ending, and Din, which is masculine.

The sixth, Tifaret, is feminine.

The seventh, eighth, and ninth—Netsach, Hod, and Yesod—are all masculine.

The tenth, Malkut, is feminine.

Thus, the ten sefirot, when viewed according to noun gender, are four female, four male, and two male-female.

What are we to make of this?

First, as we can easily count, there is now a very clear gender balance, in contrast to the traditional interpretation which is unbalanced in favor of the male. But this is only the beginning.

In traditional Kabbalah, it is not only the Tree and the paths leading from one sefirah to another that are important, but also the three "pillars"—that is, the vertical lines of sefirot. The right pillar, headed by Hokmah, has on it three sefirot that are all male in Kabbalah; in Qabalah they are male, male, female. The middle pillar is headed by Keter, in Kabbalah an ungendered sefirah with masculine undertones whose image in Qabalah becomes fully male. The other three sefirot on the middle pillar are male, male, and female. The left pillar is headed by Binah; in Kabbalah the gender of the sefirot on this pillar are female, female, male; in Qabalah they are female, male, hermaphrodite. Thus, the traditional gender representations in terms of the three pillars also make an unbalanced pattern.

However, when we look at these pillars with reformed sefirotic gender recognition, we see that each of them is balanced between female and male. The two outside pillars each start with a female sefirah and then alternate female-male, male. The center pillar begins with the male, and alternates female,

male, female. Such a balanced pattern certainly points to original intent, rather than accident. It also negates the need for achieving balance between two poles of opposites. The reformed pillars picture balance already existing on each pillar and in the whole.

What about meanings and interpretations?

Accepting the tradition that the Tree glyph which grew into Kabbalah goes back to the beginning of human history, we can assume that the form of spirituality from which it sprung is prepatriarchal. We know that Kabbalah has undergone continuing change from as far back as we can trace it up to the present time. As we have seen, these interpretations have, over thousands of years, heaped all sorts of symbols, representations, and rituals upon the Tree until it seems like an overly decorated "Christmas" tree—glitzy but with true meaning obscured.

What we need to do in contemplating the Tree, therefore, is to undergo a process similar to that of Inanna who, in her underworld visit, removed her jewels, her robes, her clothes until she stood naked to discover her real self. Just so with the Tree: to find its true form we must first remove the embellishments of patriarchal centuries, until it stands bare before us, revealing its true shape and inner meaning. When this is done, when we strip off these ornaments—when we peel away the layers of multiple meanings—what we receive from ancient times is a clear picture of prepatriarchal divinity and a possible model for modern matrifocal mysticism.

For example, the simple and obvious restoration of Hokmah (Wisdom) to its feminine gender, reveals that the first manifestation of light (or first personification or concrete image of the divine) is female. This obvious original intent was intolerable to encroaching patriarchy, so the patriarchs reversed the gender of Hokmah to hide it. (How nicely this dovetails with the traditional belief that the real meaning of Kabbalah is hidden!)

The sefirah Binah (Understanding) is also female, another aspect of the Goddess. From the traditional depiction of Binah as divided—either into virgin and warrior or bright goddess and the dark goddess—we might speculate that at one time Binah alone represented the bright aspect—or what we know as the Virgin or Maiden—and Hokmah represented the aspect we call Crone, whose primary attribute is wisdom, and who is also sometimes characterized as "dark" and having destructive traits. However, the Goddess's darkness and destruction are not evil; rather, they are necessary parts of the natural cycle of the creative process.

What of the first sefirah, Keter, being a male noun? Several explanations should be considered. First, using the term Keter for the first sefirah is a change from the original as the first sefirah was at one time called Ru'ah, a feminine noun meaning spirit. One option, to restore Ru'ah as the name of the first sefirah, does away with the monarchy of the crown and literally restores the spirit of the first sefirah. Though gendered female, we can understand this sefirah to be undifferentiated in terms of gender. Da'at (the uncounted sefirah between Hokmah/Binah and Hesed/Gevurah), is a female noun meaning knowledge; it is "invisible" in Qabalah, and in Kabbalah it is the sefirah through which we can know Keter and can therefore be considered synonymous with Keter. The manifestation of Da'at can be seen as a subconscious (or supraconscious) assertion of the (feminine) spirit of Ru'ah to the first sefirah. Taking these factors into account, we can consider the first sefirah (perhaps renamed Keter-Ru'ah) to be any or all of the following:

❀ both masculine and feminine, in an undifferentiated way
❀ ungendered but more metaphorically feminine than masculine

❀ beyond gender but containing the potential for both male and female
❀ capable of being imaged as ungendered, or as female or male, depending on the context.

Second, the traditional view of the Tree as a hierarchy with Keter "on top" may be a patriarchal concept (in fact, at least one Jewish interpretation envisions the sefirot as concentric circles)[6] that was not part of the original interpretation. Third, the original formulation may have taken place at a time when patriarchy was just beginning to make inroads in Goddess religions (similar to the time of the Innana-Damuzi myths in which Innana, although a powerful Goddess, nonetheless derives her power from a father-god). Third, Keter, even when imaged as completely masculine, is balanced by the tenth sefirah, Malkut, which in Jewish Kabbalah is also named "diadem," a synonym for crown, implying equality and union of the first and last sefirot.

The seemingly puzzling situation in the next pair of sefirot, Hesed-Gedullah and Gevurah-Din, in which each sefirah has both masculine and feminine names, I believe has a rather simple explanation. The dual gender indicates a point of transformation, and possibly also a point of union. In Qabalah, as we've noted, these sefirot are both imaged as male and it is the next trinity of sefirot (Netsach, Hod, Yesod) that involve (a rather confused and unclear) gender duality.

Dion Fortune proposes that at least part of the symbolic meaning of these three sefirot is that this is the level of magic and psychic work, which cannot be separated from sexuality. So in Qabalah, Netsach/Hod/Yesod is the plane of transformation. But from our gender analysis we can infer that the likelier original area of transformation is the preceding pair of sefirot. As we have seen, Lurianic Kabbalah teaches that sefirotic function was demoted one level after the cosmic catastrophe known as "the breaking of the vessels." We can interpret this to mean that the activities accomplished at the Netsach/Hod/Yesod level after the catastrophe, had originally been accomplished at the Hesed/Gevurah level before the calamity of suppressed Goddess worship. This verifies that in the original, Goddess-centered view of the Tree, it is the area of Hesed-Gedullah and Gevurah-Din that was the point of transformation, brought about (or aided) by sexual union—similar to the role of sex in Wiccan magic and other traditions. This energy is then channeled through Tifaret, female as indicated by its noun gender, which births the three masculine-nouned sefirot: Hod, Netsach, and Yesod. The entire Tree is rooted in Malkut, the Earth Mother.

Traditional Kabbalah speaks of three triangles on the Tree (Keter/Hokmah/Binah, Hesed/Gevurah/Tifaret, Netsach/Hod/Yesod). This scheme leaves out Malkut (the Shekinah, who, in traditional Kabbalah, has been exiled from divinity along with her people as a result of Adam's "sin").

Our analysis by noun gender, however, reveals larger triangles—a double triangle (or six-pointed star) encompassing the entire Tree. The downward-pointing triangle is composed of what we now recognize as the three female sefirot: Hokmah, Binah, and Malkut, which might be seen as corresponding to the Crone, Maiden, and Mother. The upward-pointing triangle is composed of three male sefirot: Keter, Hod, and Netsach, which might be personified as Father, Son, and Consort. Combined, the triangles form a symbol of perfect union encompassing the Tree—the aim of much of kabbalistic work. This is the union that existed before patriarchy. It was the suppression and distortion of the female divine that rented this union asunder. And it is the re-visioning of the Tree that reunites the female and male in perfect equality and harmony.

This re-visioning also speaks to another troubling aspect of Kabbalah/Qabalah: its overwhelming heterosexuality that results, at least in some forms and by some kabbalists/qabalists, to a condemnation of homosexuality. As we have said, the aim of kabbalistic spiritual work was divine heterosexual union aided by human heterosexual coitus. In Qabalah, it is balance between male and female that is the stated goal, with sexes seen as opposing forces in need of moderation.

Examining the re-visioned Tree, however, we can see that the potential for homosexual relationships exists along with the affirmation of heterosexual union. For example, the pairing of the female Hokmah and Binah or the triplicity of Hokmah/Binah/Malkut can be seen as emphasizing the bond between women, which may include sexual energy. Similarly, the male pairing of Netsach and Hod, or the triplicity of Netsach/Hod/Yesod may represent a similar bonding and energy among men. A similar interpretation can be given to the dual-gendered sefirot Hesed-Gedullah and Gevurah-Din; or they may be seen as including bisexuality. These inclusions and interpretations are substantiated in this re-visioned Tree, as the body of the Goddess includes all, and the Goddess blesses all nonexploitative manifestations of love.

Having looked at some possible new symbolism for parts of the Tree, let's look at the Tree as a whole. What is that picture really showing us?

What we have learned thus far affirms that the Tree glyph—sometimes described as having a serpent winding around it—has its roots in Goddess symbolism. While it is referred to as "the Tree," in most kabbalist drawings it hardly resembles a real tree, confirming that patriarchy changed it both graphically and symbolically beyond recognition.

The Tree is of course a universal symbol of the Goddess, as is the serpent. Further, the tree was a symbol of the Canaanite/Hebrew Goddess, Asherah.

In another possible interpretation, when drawn with the traditional Qabalah paths, which end in the double downward-pointing triangles of Netsach/Hod/Yesod and Netsach/Hod/Malkut, the glyph can be seen to resemble the snake-headed Nile River Goddess, whose legs terminate to form a glorious second yoni.

Though traditional Kabbalah often views the paths and sefirot as the body of the primordial man, Adam Kadmon, what it originally represented was the Great Mother Goddess, whose head is Keter-Ru'ah; breasts, Binah and Hokmah; hands, Hesed and Gevurah; navel or solar plexus, Tifaret; who carries in her womb her son (formed by the male sefirot Netsach, Hod, and Yesod), and whose feet are earthed in Malkut. What better symbol for the creation of the universe—the traditional subject of Kabbalah—than the pregnant Goddess?

These are just a few of the interpretations made possible by re-visioning Kabbalah (and Qabalah) according to Hebrew noun gender. They are offered here not as dogma, but as alternatives to traditional interpretations and as stepping stones to further discoveries. Kabbalah thus becomes one more facet of our spiritual heritage that when reexamined reveals a female-focal orientation and gives us a fertile field for future feminist mysticism—which I urge others to join me in exploring.

Exploring Re-Visioned Kabbalah: Meditations and Rituals

Ritual Purification of the Tree

This ritual needs to be performed only once by a group or individual. Especially good times for this are February 2 (Candlemas or Brigid), during the Jewish High Holy Days, or on any holiday related to trees. Yet any time is fine, as the spirit guides.

If you can do this ritual outside, perform it around a tree. If a bare deciduous tree is not available, choose an evergreen. Before the ritual, hang or place on the tree limbs ornaments representing kabbalistic/qabalistic reversals and other misinterpretations. Around the bottom of the tree place fruit, including apples and pomegranates, if possible. Wrap the fruit in a white cloth, so that it is fully covered.

If inside, there are several options:

❀ use an artificial Christmas tree instead of the out door tree

❀ use one or more curved-branched candelabras that allow you to use ten candles total

❀ or arrange ten candles (votive work best) in the shape of the Tree, with the candles representing the ten sefirot.

If you use candles, at the beginning of the ritual the candles are unlit and each wick (or votive glass) is covered by an "ornament." It's best that these are handmade before the ritual so that they are the appropriate size and shape for the candles. Place the fruit that is wrapped in a white cloth around the candles in a circle. (Cast circle or not, as is your custom or preference.)

Invocation

If done in a group, form a circle around the tree or altar and join hands. If you are doing this ritual alone, substitute "I" for "we" and "me" for "us."

"We come to purify the Tree, your sacred symbol: Great Goddess (or your own term for the female divine), be here with us now, purify us, and bless us in this work. So be it."

Directions

Remove the ornaments one by one, saying words appropriate to each sefirah. After each removal and words, a bell may be rung or one beat sounded on a deep-voiced drum, or "gregers" (noisemakers used on the Jewish holiday of Purim) whirled. If this ritual is done by a group, each ornament is removed by a different participant. That participant can speak the words alone, or the whole group can speak together, substituting "we" for "I." The words used may be your own, but here are some suggestions:

"I remove from the sacred Tree the false image of Keter as a bearded King.

"I remove from the sacred Tree the image of Hokmah, Wisdom, as male."

". . . the assignment of evil to Binah.

". . . the image of Hesed as a patriarchal king.

". . . the image of Gevurah as a warrior king (or the assignment of evil to Gevurah).

". . . the assignment of maleness to Tifaret.

". . . the symbolism of Venus to Netsach.

". . . the symbolism of a hermaphrodite to Hod.

". . . the implication in Yesod that all sexuality is male-centered.

". . . all association with sin and evil—and all limitations—from Malkut, the Shekinah.

When all ornaments are removed, the individual, or all present if done in a group, says:

"I (We) banish from the Tree all patriarchal distortion."

The ornaments are burned or discarded.

Purification with Salt Water

If done by a group, a container of salt water is passed to the right around the circle. Each person purifies themselves by touching salt water to whichever area(s) of their body they feel appropriate and saying: **"I am purified for this new work."**

Then, using a second container of salt water, purify the Tree (if candles are used, avoid sprinkling the wicks), and speak these words:

"I (We) purify this Tree from the taint of patriarchal reversals and distortions, and rededicate it to the work of the Goddess."

Tree Blessing

These words are then spoken:

"Sacred Tree,
restored now to the beauty of nature
rooted again in the richness of earth
May your limbs blossom
with the flower of love.
May your branches brim with
the fruit of labor.
May we discover your secrets in openness.
May we know your truths with pleasure.
And may all your paths bring peace.
So be it."

Re-Visioning

Begin by saying: "With these words we (I) re-vision the Tree."

If using candles, each candle is lit, one at a time, with the person lighting the candle saying the Hebrew name of the sefirah and a word or symbol appropriate to its re-visioning. As the words are spoken, an individual, or the whole group, walks to the left around the tree. Examples:

Malkut: Mother Earth, Mother of all; Root of being.
Yesod: Her Son the Father.
Hod: Child, brother.
Netsach: Lover, partner, friend.
Tifaret: Healing beauty of the Goddess in nature; indwelling divine presence; core of being.

Gevurah/Din: Woman of valor; lawgiver; transformative power; sacred sex; magic.

Hesed/Gedullah: Kind man; counselor; transmutation of energy; divine intuition.

Binah: Bright and pure understanding; sacred Maiden.

Hokmah: First manifestation; ancient Crone called Wisdom.

Keter-Ru'ah: Spirit; undifferentiated light; eternal becoming.

Guided Meditation

Done seated. Close your eyes. Relax and breathe slowly and deeply, taking three long breaths. Now take three breaths, slowly and deeply and on each exhalation, as you breathe out, say "Kab-ba-lah" in three even syllables.

Continue now, breathing slowly and gently until you see a tree, a tree in full bloom. On its branches are ten pieces of fruit. They can be any type of fruit that you like. (Pause) Watch now, as each piece of fruit starts shining, perhaps from the glint of the sun, perhaps from the glow of the moon, or perhaps from some inner light. Continue to watch as the each fruit becomes a circle of shining shimmering light. (Pause)

And as you continue to watch, the shining shimmering circles begin to move. (Pause) And as they move, they begin to form patterns, new patterns. (Pause)

As you watch them move and change, ask now for these lights to show you the secret meaning of the Tree, the meaning that you receive from ancient times; the special meaning that the Tree has for you. Watch the lights, as they move and change and see what answer they give you. They may form an image, or write a word. Or you may just get a feeling from watching them. They may remain separate lights, become more lights, or grow into one light. Receive now, the meaning of the Tree. (Long pause)

Now that you have received the meaning of the Tree, let the lights again form into ten distinct lights. (Pause) And now, let them become fruit again, and see them again on the Tree. (Pause)

Now let your breathing become strong again, taking three deep breaths and then on three more breaths, breathe "Kabba-lah" on the exhales. (Pause as this is done.) Now slowly open your eyes and come back to this time and place.

Nourishment

Uncover fruit saying:

"This fruit symbolizes the fruit that shall come from the re- visioned Tree. Let us eat and be nourished."

(Eat fruit)

Closing Blessing

If done in a group, stand in a circle. This can be done antiphonally, with one section saying the blessed be's and the others responding with the end of the sentences; or all can say the blessed be's and individuals can say the ends of the various lines, with people adding more lines, if they wish.

Blessed be that which we receive from ancient times.
Blessed be that which we recreate.
Blessed be that which we create anew.
Blessed be the Tree of nature.
Blessed be the Tree of life.
Blessed be the Tree of knowledge.
Blessed be the created and the creator.
Blessed be.

SEFIROT MEDITATIONS

Now we explore the Tree relieved of hierarchy. The meditations begin here with Malkut because it is the root from which the Tree grows. Most people will want to start at Malkut and climb the Tree limb by limb, experiencing each sefirah, with Keter-Ru'ah last. But this is not a hard-and-fast rule. You can chose another place to start, the place you feel is appropriate for you. For example, if your most intense spiritual pursuit is now magic, you may want to start at Gevurah; if psychic, at Hesed. If you are male, or are most used to imaging divinity as only male, it may be easiest to start at Yesod. If you never use gendered images or pronouns when speaking about divinity, you may want to start at Keter-Ru'ah. If you feel you need healing before proceeding with spiritual work, it may help to start at Tifaret.

Each sefirah is necessary to the entire Tree; each aspect of divinity is necessary to the whole; each experience of divinity is necessary to comprehending the whole; each quality is necessary to the whole person.

Just as you would climb up, down, and around a tree, moving from limb to limb, so after you have completed a meditation on one sefirah, travel along the branches (channels, paths) to the next nearest sefirah until you have incorporated all of them into your spiritual thinking and practices.

It is suggested that you do no more than one meditation a week, repeating it daily if you wish, so that you fully absorb the material.

These meditations can be done alone or in a group. You should be seated, with both feet on the floor, and your hands on your lap, eyes closed. Begin each meditation by breathing fully and deeply until you reach a state of quiet relaxation.

Malkut

Visualize the color brown, the color of the earth beneath our feet. And from this color let coalesce an area of blue, the color of Earth when seen from outer space. (Pause) Let it form into an orb, a spinning sphere, containing brown and green, with mountains and valleys and deserts; with oceans, rivers, and streams; with grasses, flowers, and trees. (Short pause)

And now go to that spinning sphere, be on that globe, and find a place with trees. Perhaps it is a place you have been before, or perhaps a place you have always wanted to go. Or even a place that exists only in your imagination. Go now to this place of trees. (Pause)

Take a while to walk in this place, to feel the earth under your feet, to enjoy the trees. (Pause) Now you see a tree that appeals to you more than the others. It may be right in front of you, or behind you. Or it may be down the path some distance ahead. Go to that tree now. (Pause)

And when you get to the tree, sit down under it, your back against its trunk, and relax. (Pause) And as you sit under the tree, a woman appears in the distance. She wears only a sky-blue cape edged with brown. She is carrying a basket. As she comes closer, notice the color of her skin, her hair, her eyes. How tall is she? What are her other physical characteristics? (Pause)

She is singing a song as she approaches. You can hear the song now. Listen, so that you can remember her song. (Pause)

When she reaches you, she sits down beside you and opens her basket, taking from it a flower. She smells the flower, then gives it to you, asking you to smell it too. You take the flower. What color is it? What sort of scent does it have? (Pause)

Now she takes from her basket some food and gives some to you and some to herself. You both eat. What kind of food is it? How does it taste? (Pause)

And now that you are finished eating, she reaches for your hand and you feel it enclose yours. How does it feel? (Pause) And now, if you wish, she hugs you, perhaps she even kisses you. Or she may simply continue to hold your hand. (Pause) And now, if you want, close your eyes and allow her touch to warm you, to encompass you until you feel the separation between the woman and you melting away. This feeling can come simply by holding her hand, if you prefer. (Pause) Now, if you like, allow yourself to merge with this woman; allow yourself to feel all she can give you, allow yourself to feel all you can become. (Long pause)

Now, still under your tree, imagine yourself opening your eyes, and when you do, the woman is nowhere to be seen. Yet you feel she is still with you. She has left her basket for you to take home with you. You open the basket and there is one last thing in it, her gift to you. What is it? (Pause)

Now you get up, taking the basket and her gift with you, and walk down the path until you reach this time and place. When you do, slowly open your eyes.

Yesod

Visualize the color green in front of your closed eyes. As your breathing becomes still, let the green coalesce into an orb, a green orb, which may be surrounded by blue, the blue of the sky. Go towards the green orb now, and as you do, you see it get larger and larger (short pause) until you are surrounded by its green. (Pause) And now the green becomes a landscape with a field of green grass. You move into the landscape now and stand in the middle of the field. Perhaps there are flowers growing there. Or vegetables. (Pause) It is just before sunrise, and you see the dew on the plants and feel the cool breeze. You notice a stream flowing through the middle of the field, and in the distance, a tree. (Pause)

Now, as the sun comes up, it quickly becomes hot. (Short pause) You go to the stream for a sip of water, but you see dead minnows floating on the top of the water. You dip your hands in the water, hoping to cool off that way, but your hands sting, then burn—from the chemicals that have polluted the water. (Pause)

The heat continues. It is so hot the grass starts to turn brown and the plants begin to wither. When you look again at the stream, it has dried up, revealing more dead fish and also trash.

The heat has tired you, so you lie down on the browning grass, midst the shriveled plants, and drift off to sleep. But you do not dream. (Short pause) It seems you have been sleeping only an instant, but when you wake up, with the sun still overhead, the vegetation has vanished and you are lying on cracked, parched earth. You get up and start towards the tree, hoping for shade. But as you approach, you see its leaves are gone and some of its branches have broken off.

How does this make you feel? (Pause)

You are just about to turn and head back in the other direction, when you see a man emerge from the center of the tree. He wears only a green cloak. As he comes toward you, you see that his hair is green too, like blades of grass.

What else do you notice about him? (Pause)

"Why is the earth drying up?" you ask him.

What is his reply?

He also says that he can repair the damage if you will help him and then he begins dancing. As he dances, his green cloak gets longer and longer as he whirls round and round; longer and longer grows his cloak until it covers the earth; longer and wider it becomes as it covers the stream; longer and wider and higher it grows as he whirls and his cloak covers the tree. And finally, you too are enfolded in his green cloak, dancing his dance with him. (Short pause) As you dance, he begins singing a song of love to Earth. As you dance, his song dances in your ears. (Pause) Can you understand the words? (Pause) Can you join in the singing? (Pause)

As the dancing and singing continue, a fine mist of rain cools and refreshes you. And the grass begins to sprout. After more whirling, exhausted, you both fall to the ground, to Earth, now green once more. On the blanket of the green Earth you fall into a deep sleep, and this time you dream. What do you dream? (Long pause)

Now you awake and as you awake you see the green man is gone. But the flowers are blooming and the crops are growing so fast you can watch them rise up. And the tree once again is heavy with green leaves.

You walk past the tree, peeking in the hollow of the trunk— but see no one. You continue on a path that brings you back to this time and place and you bring back with you his words, his dance, his song, and your dream. And now you slowly open your eyes.

Hod

As you close your eyes, you see a yellow ball; it moves, bounces in front of your eyes as if it were a rubber ball being bounced by a child. Watch as the yellow ball bounces playfully before your eyes. (Pause)

As the ball continues to bounce, you see a pudgy hand bouncing it, a child's hand. (Pause)

And now you see the little boy who's bouncing the ball. How old does he look? (Pause)

And now the boy bounces the ball to you. Can you catch it? (Pause)

You get the ball. You take it in your hands. How does it feel? (Pause) What do you want to do with it? (Pause)

The boy calls to you to throw him the ball. What do you do? (Pause)

Now the boy has the yellow ball again. And he throws you another ball. What color is it? (Pause)

You can do anything you want to with this ball. What do you do? (Long pause)

Now the boy asks you to play a game with him. It can be any kind of game that you want. If you need more children for the game, he will get some friends.

Now you can play any game you want. What do you do? (Long pause) Something happens in the game that is funny. What is it? (Pause) The boy laughs and laughs and when you hear him laugh it makes you laugh. Laughing makes you feel happy and free. (Pause)

Now you hear some other laughing, the laughter of a grown-up woman. (Short pause) And then you see the boy's mother coming out into the yard with a snack for you—yellow pears. The boy grabs a pear and takes a big bite, the juice dribbling down his chin. Now you take a pear. You take a bite. How does it taste? How does it feel in your mouth? (Pause)

Now you hear a voice calling your name. It's not the boy's voice, and it's not his mother's voice. Whose voice is it? (Pause)

You know what the voice means. It's time to go home—it's time to come back to this time and place. But you can bring with you the playfulness and laughter that you shared with the boy.

Netsach

As you close your eyes, across a field of black you see an orange orb. (Pause) As you look at the orange orb, you think of a secret problem that you have been trying to deal with. A problem that involves forgiveness. (Pause)

As you think of your problem and watch the orange orb, the orb begins tumbling towards you. (Pause) As it gets closer, you can see from the roughness of its skin that it is an orange, a piece of fruit.

The tumbling fruit distracts you from your problem, and you reach out for the orange, but when you do it begins rolling away from you. You follow it into the darkness, you follow the orange because it looks so delicious. You follow the orange into the dark, but the orange disappears and in a burst of light you find yourself in another place: a place where friends can meet and have a quiet conversation. (Pause) It may be a place from this time or from another century, past or future, or it may be a time out of time. It may be somewhere you have been before, or an entirely new place. (Pause)

At this place, you find a friend waiting for you: a young man who seems quite familiar to you, even if you have never seen him before. He is dressed all in black but for an orange sweater or other type of orange outer garment appropriate for the time and place. You sit down with your friend and chat lightly for a few minutes. What do you talk about? (Pause)

As you continue to chat, you come to feel that you can tell this friend anything and he will not condemn you. You know that he accepts you and that nothing you could do or say would shock him and that he will always remain your friend.

So you decide to tell him your secret. You decide to tell him about your problem that involves the need for forgiveness—either for something you did, or for you to forgive something that someone else did. You remember how it all started and you feel the anguish this secret gives you, (pause) and you know you want help getting rid of it. So in perfect trust, you tell your friend this secret now. (Long pause)

After you finish telling your secret, your friend, very sympathetically, says something to you. What does he say? (Pause)

And now your friend asks you if you want to receive forgiveness, or to forgive, whichever is appropriate. And you answer. (Pause)

And now your friend suggests what to do to attain forgiveness. Listen carefully now to what he says. (Pause)

It's up to you whether to follow his suggestion, for you know best what is the right thing for you. His suggestion may have given you an idea of what to do that differs from what he suggests. You can do what he suggests or what you have thought of; you can do it now, or later, or not at all, whatever you decide. (Long pause)

And now your friend reaches into the pocket of his orange outer garment and brings out the orange fruit you were pursuing before. He holds it out to you in perfect love, and you take it. You can eat it now, or later, or never—it's up to you. (Pause)

And now you tell your friend that it's time for you to go. You thank him for his help and for the orange. And you come back to this place and time.

Tifaret

Close your eyes and relax. Let your breathing become especially deep and slow and relaxing. Relax, beginning with your feet and moving upward, take time now, as you breath slowly, easily, and deeply, to let every part of your body relax. (Long pause)

And as your body relaxes, you see an orb of purple in your special inner vision. It may be a very tiny orb. Or it may be a very large orb. It can be any size. And as you watch this purple orb, it takes on a luminescence, it shines with an inner light. Take a moment now to enjoy its beautiful purple glow. (Pause)

And now you see that the purple orb, shining like a star, begins to move, and you follow the orb, you follow the purple star to see where it will lead, knowing that wherever it takes you will be a safe, loving place. (Short pause)

And you follow the purple star to a stairway that leads down into the earth. And with the purple star now directly in front of you, you step on the first step down, which is of earth, of clay, and then on the second step down, which is of stone, of granite, and then three more steps down to the first landing. As you descend those three steps, notice what they are made of. (Pause)

And now you follow the purple star down the second flight of stairs. And these stairs are all of quartz, the first few clear quartz crystal, then citrine, aventurine, onyx, carnelian and rose quartz—until finally you reach the last few steps which are of amethyst. (Short pause)

And when you get to the bottom of the stairs, you are standing in an amethyst grotto. And your purple star blends into the walls and rounded ceiling of amethyst crystal—of all colors from dark purple to lavender to pink-lavender to almost clear. Take a moment to look around this beautiful glowing amethyst temple. (Pause)

And now from the other end of the grotto, a figure enters surrounded, it seems, by a purple cloud. And as you look at this figure coming towards you, wonder fills you, and fear vanishes. (Pause)

And as the figure approaches closer, you realize that what looked like a cloud is actually the flowing garment, veil upon veil of purple, which clothes this beautiful person, whose face is also veiled in purple. (Short pause) She stands in front of you now and removes the veil from her face and you look into her eyes. (Pause)

She smiles and indicates a place where you can sit. You sit. (Short pause) And now that you are sitting, you notice that a small rivulet, a tiny stream makes its way along the amethyst floor, passing right in front of your feet. (Pause)

And while you have been looking at the stream, the beautiful woman in purple has lit white candles in a circle around you and you see them shine and you watch as their light increases the light of the amethyst around, below, and above you. (Pause)

And now the woman stands in front of you, the rivulet running between her feet and yours, and she removes a transparent veil that winds from her shoulders to her knees. Yet underneath the veil, the woman remains clothed in beautiful, flowing satin purple. And she asks you if you would like to wear her veil around your shoulders while you are here. How do you reply? (Pause)

She responds to your reply and then stands in front of you. She extends her arms, palms up, towards the ceiling of amethyst, and as she does so, light begins emanating from her hands. What color is the light? (Pause)

And now she turns her palms so that they are towards you, and the color emanating from her palms becomes the color that you need to heal your physical body. What color is it? (Pause)

And now you feel the warmth of this healing entering your body wherever you need healing. Relax now, and let this beautiful healing enter your body, wherever it is needed, in the exact amount it is needed, and know that you are fully and completely protected. (Long pause)

And now you see emanating from the woman's heart, light of the color that you need to heal your emotions. What color is the light? (Pause) And now you breathe in this light, you relax, and you let this light heal your emotions, going as deeply as it needs to go to accomplish this healing, in the exact amount that is needed, in a way that is always comfortable, and comforting for you. And you know that as this healing takes place, you are fully and completely protected. (Long pause)

And now the light emanates from the woman's entire body. It may be light of one color or of many colors. As you see the lights now, know that this is the energy that you need to receive healing of the spirit. And the woman asks you if would like to receive this healing now, and you answer. (Pause)

If you said you do not feel that this healing is appropriate for you now, then you sit quietly in the glow of the circle of candles, in the glow of amethyst, and know that this healing will be available to you whenever you feel it is appropriate.

If you told the woman that you are ready for healing of the spirit, then relax and be open to this healing which emanates to you now from the body of beauty which is the woman; this healing emanates to you in the colors of light that you need, in the exact amount that you need, and in a way that is fulfilling for you. And know that as you receive this healing you are fully and completely protected. (Long pause)

And now the woman indicates to you that it is time for her to leave. She replaces her veils, and glides away from you towards the innermost part of the amethyst grotto, and you watch her depart in a purple cloud.

And just as the purple cloud goes out of sight, a short but strong wind blows out the candles, and the purple star reappears once again in front of you. And you follow it out of the grotto, up the flight of crystal steps—as slowly or as quickly as you like—then to the landing, then up the second flight of steps—at your own speed—and, when you are ready, back to this place and time.

Gevurah/Din

As you close your eyes you see an orb. Half of the orb is red and half of it is teal—a deep greenish blue. As you look at the orb—half red, half teal—it may begin to change size, or shape; one color may take up more of the orb than the other, or it may become all one color and then all the other color. Watch now as the orb changes in front of your eyes. (Pause)

You move now towards the orb, and as you do, it becomes bigger but also its colors begin to get less intense. And as you continue to approach, it continues to get bigger, taking up all your vision now, until you realize that without even trying you are inside the orb. The red has faded to a steamy mist, and the teal runs through the lush vegetation that surrounds you. It is so warm, so steamy and so lovely in this place that you at once feel very relaxed, and even a little lethargic. You walk a little ways, passing a stream curving languorously through the rich vegetation, until you come to a place where there is a hammock hung between strong tall trees. You want to lie down in the hammock, but you are also very warm, so you take off some of your clothes. Take off only what you want to, what makes you feel more comfortable. You also take out of one of your pockets an object you have brought with you. The object represents something in your life that you want to change—it may be something about yourself, or something about a relationship. Look at the object now and notice every detail about it. (Pause) You have brought this symbol hoping you will be able to find a way here to change this aspect of your life. You hold it in your hand now as you lie down in the hammock and swing slowly, slowly in the hammock. Enjoy the swinging now as it lulls you. (Pause)

And as you swing in the hammock, your mind loosens, becomes freer, until it seems it can flow freely from place to place, object to object, and you find that if you look at a plant that is red and want it to be yellow, it will change to yellow. And if you want to change the course of the stream a bit, so will it be, as long as it poses no threat to what surrounds it. Let your eyes move now through the scene around you, and if you want something to change, ask it to change and watch what happens. (Pause)

And now you turn your attention to the object you have brought with you that you still hold in your hands, the object that represents something in your life you want to change. And now you ask it to change, but it doesn't. It remains the same. You are disappointed, but the feeling lasts only an instant as you are lulled again by the swinging, swinging of the hammock. You get drowsy now, and are just about to drift off to sleep when you see a figure coming towards you, rising from the mist in this lush, steamy place. At first, seen at the distance, it looks like one large figure swathed in red and teal, flowing first here, then there in the steamy mist. (Pause) But now as the figure gets closer and closer, you see it as two distinct beings: a man in a transparent garment of teal edged with red and a woman in a transparent gown of red edged with teal. They are both very physically attractive. What else can you see about them as they draw closer? (Pause)

And now they stand next to your hammock. They are both very lovely, with the light of their garments emanating all around them. You feel yourself drawn to one more than the other. The attraction is spiritual and erotic, both at the same time. Reach now for the hand of the one to whom you are most strongly attracted. (Pause)

The one whose hand you have taken sits on the hammock next to you. And you give to this one the object you have brought with you, the object symbolizing something in your life you want to change. As you remain lying in the hammock, the one you have chosen hands the object to the other one, who takes it and stands now behind your head, guarding you and keeping you safe. Sense the protection that figure is giving you now. (Pause)

Now the one you are most attracted to, the one you have chosen, lies down beside you and you embrace. And you are completely in control of what happens next as you continue to embrace and love one another. (One- to three-minute pause)

You come out of the embrace now and the one you have loved rises from the hammock and you sit up in the hammock, your feet over the side, touching the moist earth. The one who has protected you comes from behind the hammock to stand in front of you now and extends to you your symbol. You take it and see at once that the object has changed. How does it look now? (Pause)

This change symbolizes the change you want in your life. You look up from your object just as the two figures are receding into the mist, merging again into one large fluid figure, and you come to understand how to bring about the change you desire in your life. (Pause)

You bring this knowledge back with you now, as you return to this time and place.

Hesed/Gedullah

Close your eyes and as you breathe deeply and relax, think of a question you would like answered: Something you would like to know about yourself, your future, or your relationships, perhaps about your career or finances or the direction your life might take. (Pause) And as you think of this question, you see in front of you an orb either of reddish orange or of aqua, or of both. Whichever way the orb appears to you is right for you. And now watch as the words of your question, or a picture or symbol about that question, appear on the orb. Where the orb is reddish orange, the question appears in aqua; where the orb is aqua, the question appears in reddish orange. (Pause)

And now watch as the words or image fade into the reddish-orange and aqua orb. And as this happens, as the word or image fade, the orb begins glowing more brightly. You can feel the warmth from that glow, a warmth like love and you feel drawn to it. And so you move toward the orb, and at the same time it moves toward you, growing larger until it surrounds you, and you are floating as if in a large balloon. And as you float in this balloon of light, you feel safe and loved. (Pause)

And now as you float in the balloon, you see three chairs facing one another in a small circle in front of you. One chair is aqua, one reddish orange, and one is both colors. You pick one of the chairs and sit down. (Pause) And when you are sitting down, two figures enter: one, a male, in a lavish aqua robe trimmed with orange and red; and the other, a female, in a lavish orange-red robe with aqua trim. And you feel emanating from them the same love you felt from the orb, only now it has become even stronger and more unconditional. (Pause)

And now the man and woman sit down in the chairs facing you. Which color chairs do they pick? (Pause)

And now the three of you, seated on your chairs, join hands in a circle, and as you do, you feel as if a gentle current of electricity is passing among you, through your joined hands. (Pause)

And now you gently drop their hands and place your hands on your lap—yet you can still feel the current that connects you. (Pause) And as you continue sitting, you feel the connection with one of the persons—either the woman or the man—is stronger than with the other. And as you continue to feel this connection, though no words are spoken, thoughts begin to pass between you and this other person. This flow of thoughts goes beyond reading each others minds, for it seems the thoughts are coming into both your minds at the same time. And as this happens, protection emanates from the third person; it may emanate as wings or as light, and it spreads to protect you and the person with whom you are communicating so that you continue to feel safe and loved. (Pause)

And now, feeling completely safe and loved, you ask your question of the person with whom you have been communicating, the one with whom your connection is the strongest. You ask it now. (Pause)

And you receive the answer immediately. (Pause)

And now you thank the person for helping you find the answer. (Pause) And you thank the other person for protecting you. (Pause) And you thank them both for their love. (Pause)

And keeping the feeling of unconditional love within you, know that it is yours always. And now, in a way that is comfortable for you, come back to this place and time.

Binah

As you close your eyes and relax, out of the darkness arises a silver-white orb. Its light is like the light of the moon and it shines on you now. (Pause)

And as the light shines on you, as you feel its energy, you see it form into a waxing crescent moon, the early light of illumination. And as you see this crescent, as you feel the energy of this new light, you think of an area, or a problem, or a subject in your life that you would like illuminated. It may be a subject you are studying that you don't quite understand; it may be another person whose actions mystify you, a person you would like to understand better; it may be an attraction to someone, or a dislike of someone that seems to have no reason, that may not be completely comfortable and you would like to know more about it. It may be any of these things, or it may be something else in your life that you need to understand. You think of it now as you continue to gaze at the silver-white light, as you continue to feel the energy of the silver-white light. (Pause)

And now, as the light continues to emanate from the crescent, slowly, slowly, the light forms a female figure; slowly, slowly, the light becomes a young woman.

You look now upon this young woman, the Maiden. (Pause)

And as you continue to look at this young woman, you are no longer aware of the crescent, but see only her. (Pause)

And now you sense her energy, the strength of the mighty Maiden. And that strength is both physical and spiritual. (Pause) She demonstrates that strength, that energy to you now. What does she do? (Pause)

And now as you continue to look at her, she may remain the same, or she may change. (Pause)

And now you bring to her attention the subject you want to understand. You bring it to her attention in your own way, in a way that is comfortable for you. (Pause)

As you bring this subject to her attention, she may change, or she may remain the same. (Pause)

And now you sense—perhaps you even see—how she is concentrating, focusing, on the subject you have brought to her. It is a concentration without strain, a focus without fear. And as she continues to focus, and you feel drawn closer and closer to her until her focus becomes your focus, and you seem to be looking at the subject through her eyes, concentrating on the subject through her mind. (Pause)

And now so easily you see the problem you have brought before her clearly, in all its ramifications, you see it more clearly than you have ever seen it before. (Pause)

And now you understand this subject, this problem, better than you ever have understood it before, for your understanding is her understanding. (Long pause) And as this understanding becomes complete, you slowly begin to separate from her, retaining your understanding. (Pause)

And as you separate from her, you see her encompassed again by white-silver light of the waxing crescent moon. (Pause) And now, as you watch, the image of the Maiden becomes smaller but the moon crescent remains, rising high above you in the sky, shining its promise upon you. (Short pause) And you know, as the light shines on you, that the understanding you have received here is only the beginning of what is possible. (Short pause)

And now you give thanks for the understanding you have received. (Pause) And still feeling the light of understanding, the light of promise, the light of beginnings, when you are ready, come back to this place and time.

Hokmah

As you close your eyes, breathe deeply and fully. As you breathe deeply and relax, you become aware of the darkness before your closed eyes. Dark as dark can get, deep as dark can go. (Pause)

And as you continue to gaze into the darkness, you begin to notice that there are variations in the darkness, some places where the darkness is darker, some where it is ever so slightly lighter. (Pause)

And as you continue looking around this variegated darkness, you realized there is shining light, a round border of light emanating from the darkness, which has now become sapphire blue: A round orb of sapphire blue shining in the dark. (Pause) And now you watch as the sapphire blue oscillates from darkest blue, to royal blue, to even lighter blue, and the back again through the various shades of blue. Watch and see all the varieties of blue that this orb has to reveal. (Pause)

And now, as the blue orb oscillates, you see emerging from the orb an ancient one, an ancient woman. (Pause) The first one. (Pause) She who was first and who is with us yet. (Pause)

She is covered from the top of her head to the bottom of her feet in sapphire blue, robe upon robe of sapphire blue, cape upon robe of sapphire blue, and on her head, a thick scarf—a babushka—of sapphire blue. (Pause)

And you go toward her now, wanting to go closer, to know her, to see her better. (Pause)

And as you continue to approach, she greets you and begins to remove her scarf from around her head. She removes it slowly. Watch now, as she removes her scarf. (Pause) And as she finishes removing her scarf, she reveals something about herself that you did not know before. There is something about her that is different now that her babushka is off. What is it?

And you see this change, and you understand this change, not only what it shows you literally, but also its true meaning. (Pause)

And now she invites you to go on a journey with her. She is going to take you with her on her travels, and you move closer and allow her to wrap you in her long flowing cape, allow her to wrap you in her long flowing robes, robe upon robe upon cape upon robe, and you go with her as she moves through that which is, as she travels through that which shall be, moving now through that which no longer is but shall be again. (Pause)

And now you stand with her in a mist, a spray mist of ocean waves. (Pause) And as you watch, the mist lifts and you clearly see the waves breaking—you see both the smooth swell of the waves before they crest and the foam and power as they break; and you sense both the ebb and the flow. (Pause) And as you watch, you know all there is to know about this scene, both the literal meaning of what you see and sense, and also the inner meaning. All is now revealed. (Pause)

And again you travel with the ancient one through that which is, through that which shall be, through that which is no more but shall be again. (Pause)

And now you stand at a top of a mountain. And the edge of the mountain is surrounded in fog. (Pause) And the wind blows and you watch now as the fog lifts. And you move with the woman out to the very edge of the mountain, to the very edge of this cliff. And the wind is calm once more. (Pause) And you look over the edge of the cliff, knowing that her wisdom protects you. (Short pause) As you look over the cliff, what do you see? (Pause) This scene becomes clearer and clearer until you can see everything there is to see about this scene, until you know all there is to know. (Pause) And you see all there is to see about the mountain and about the valley, and you sense all there is to know, both the literal meaning and the true inner meaning of what is revealed to you now. (Pause)

And now you travel again with this ancient woman whose robes shine like sapphire, whose cloak wraps you in safety. And you travel with her through that which is, through that which shall be, through that which no longer is but shall be again. (Pause)

And now you stand in the midst of smoke. Smoke that slowly evaporates until you are gazing into a bright fire. Look now at the fire, at its brightness, (pause) feel its heat, (pause) experience its power. (Pause)

And now you look into this fire, you look into the flames, and—in a way that is both literal and which also reveals a great inner meaning—you come to know all you need to know about the fire and that which is contained in the fire, in this greatest of lights. (Long pause)

And now, moving again with the woman, the ancient one, the first one, you travel back to the place where you started. (Pause) And you move outside of her robe, outside of her cloak. (Pause) And now she takes her scarf—her babushka—and wraps it once again around her head. And as she does so, she is once again as you first met her. (Pause)

And now she becomes one once again with the blue sapphire orb. (Pause)

And now, becoming aware of your breathing once more, you let the orb change back from sapphire blue to darkest of dark, still keeping within you the shining wisdom you have received. And you give thanks for this wisdom. (Pause) And you come back now, when you are ready, to this place and time.

Keter-Ru'ah

In your inner vision the dark of nothingness floats before your eyes. (Pause) Then you feel rather than see this nothingness begin to pulsate. (Pause) As it continues to pulsate, you are able to see changes in the darkness until it becomes alive with light. (Pause) And your mind empties of everything but the light, as you hear these words:

Light birthed of dark. (Pause)
Light formed of nothing. (Pause)
First light. (Pause)
Source of all. (Pause)

Word beyond words. (Long pause)
Sound beyond sound. (Long pause)
Vision without image. (Long pause)
I wait for your voice. (Pause)
I wait for your word. (Pause)
I wait for your song. (Pause)
I wait for your vision. (One- to five-minute pause)

Thank you for the flow of your light
around me and all of creation
through me and all of creation.
So be it.

PERMUTATION OF HOLY NAMES

This meditation is based on similar practices of kabbalists.
The meditator(s) should be seated.

Use Goddess names of two or three syllables (if of two syllables, add an extra syllable, as shown). All three syllables
should be accented equally, during one exhaled breath. You
will note when this is done some pronunciations change or are
exaggerated slightly.

Some examples:

Asherah (Ah-shear-ah)
Kali Ma (Ka-lee-Mah)
Astarte (A-star-tay)
Ostara (O-star-ah)
Innana (Ee-nah-nah)

For the first few times, until you get used to the energy,
this is best done with at least three people. Surround yourselves with lit votive candles, or if candles are not practical,
visualize yourselves surrounded by light.

Choose one sacred name to work with during each separate meditation.

Relax, take three deep breaths. Beginning with the fourth exhale, say the sacred name in three evenly accented syllables on one exhale. Start with everyone saying the name together, then allow everyone to breathe names as is right for them. Let the breathing of names continue until people are automatically breathing the names. When this happens the syllables may get mixed up, some may get repeated and some omitted, other sounds may be made. This is okay. The name breathing will eventually become automatic, so you are no longer aware of it, and trance is likely. When trance occurs the name breathing is likely to lessen and then end. One person, designated before as leader, should allow time for trance and then bring people back by repeating the Goddess name three times, in ordinary voice and phrasing and then saying:

"Thank you [Goddess name] for being with us here today (tonight). Thank you for the insights we have received. Thank you for bringing us closer to you."

Discuss the experience and share food.

After doing this with individual names, the group may want to try using three different Goddess names at the same time: that is, each person chooses one Goddess name from among three names the group has chosen to use. Each person breathes that one name and continues breathing that same name throughout the meditation, while others are breathing the two other Goddess names. Upon ending, thank all three Goddesses.

You may want to discuss whether the energy, experience, vision varies with the Goddess name used.

After you have had experience in the group, you may want to try this in private meditation, using one Goddess name per meditation. You need to be an experienced meditator for this and you need to be comfortable with bringing yourself back from the trance state.

FULL MOON RITUAL

Cast circle, call directions, if that is the group's preference or practice.

Invocation

Bountiful Mother
Full of light
Shine on us
This blessed night.
Maintain the balance
Of the Tree.
Sustain the union
That makes us free.
Be in our hearts,
Shining bright,
Beautiful Mother
Full of light.

Dancing

Dancing during this ritual is meant to induce a light trance. One way to do this is to begin to dance slowly, (for example, a slow hora) hands joined, moving to the left. After a few minutes, hands are dropped and individuals dance on their own. Possibilities for this include individual Kletzmer-like dancing or belly dancing, or any totally free-form individual dancing. As you begin dancing by yourself, let the music fill you and dance your own dance in response to the music. Increasingly let yourself become one with the music so that you are aware only of the music and your movement. As the dancing ends, the music should become increasingly slower.

Starting with the hora, or some other form of dance where people join hands, helps those not used to dancing get past their self-consciousness and into the rhythm of the music. However, some groups may want to skip the hands-joined dance and simply start with free-form dancing.

If your group doesn't like to dance, or if there isn't enough space, "Permutation of Holy Names" can be used to induce trance.

Guided Meditation

(Alternately, one of the separate sefirah meditations can be used.)

Eyes closed, sitting or lying down, breathe deeply to reach a relaxed state.

See all ten sefirot as shining orbs, shining on the Tree. (Pause)

As you watch, the orbs soften, coalesce into a body: the head is the orb of Keter-Ru'ah. See the head, the hair, the face of the Goddess. (Pause)

Now see her body form before your eyes, as Hokmah and Binah become her breasts; Hesed and Gevurah her hands; and Tifaret becomes her solar plexus, her navel; see how in her womb she carries Netsach, Hod, and Yesod, her son; see how she encompasses within her the male; see She who gives birth to all, She whose feet are rooted in Malkut, Earth. (Pause)

Sense this wholeness.

Sense this completeness.

Sense this fullness.

(Pause)

And now let the image of the pregnant Goddess slowly become the Tree with the ten sefirot once again. (Pause)

Now watch as the orbs of Keter, Hokmah, Binah, Hod, Netsach, and Malkut shine more brightly. (Pause) And their brightness increases until you are conscious of an increased flow of energy. Watch as the energy flows from Malkut to Binah to Hokmah and back again to Malkut in one continuous circuit of female energy. Watch the flow of energy in this large downward-pointing triangle—it may appear to flow like water or a flame, or some other sort of flowing energy. (Pause)

And, as the energy continues flowing in a circuit among Malkut, Binah, and Hokmah, see how energy also flows from Keter to Hod to Netsach in one large upward-pointing triangle, in one continuous circuit of male energy. This circuit may appear to flow like fire or water, or like something else. (Pause)

And now see the two large triangles, encompassing the entire Tree, joined in a giant six-pointed star: the reunion of female and male, in perfect love, in perfect trust, in perfect equality. In perfection. (Pause)

Feel this union.

Feel its completeness.

Feel its wholeness.

(Pause)

And now the energy of union brings the other lights on the Tree to their fullest shining. And you see ten orbs, each shining with the light of the full moon. Enjoy this light. (Pause) And now, let the Tree fade from your vision, as you bring back with you to this place and time, its completeness, its fullness, its light.

Tarot Reading

Before tarot cards are distributed, the following is said:

"Great Mother, thank you for the light that surrounds us. Thank you for guidance we receive in the protection of your light. So be it."

As the tarot deck is passed to the left, each person draws a card and looks at it, focusing with inner vision on the person on their right (who has given them the deck). When each person has a card, go around the circle, with each person giving a short reading based on the card, for the person on the right.

Song: Full Moon, Whole Moon

(Suggested music: Theme from 2nd movement of Beethoven piano sonata Op. 13 "Pathétique")

1

Full moon, whole moon
Your light my life inspires.
Make clear now
by your sphere now
all messages you send me

2

Full light, whole light
Whose vision I receive
stay with me
so I can see
Pregnant One of eternity

3

Whole tree, Holy
Your lights my life inform
In balance
And in union
May all your paths peace bring me.

Blessing

Great Goddess, in whom we are whole,
thank you for being with us tonight.
May we always be channels for your wisdom.
May we always dwell in the fullness of your Tree.
May you always guide us on your blessed paths
  of peace.
So be it.

Chapter 6
Taking the Quantum Leap

So long as the universe had a beginning, we could suppose it had a creator. But if the universe is really completely self-contained, having no boundary or edge, it would have neither beginning nor end: it would simply be. What place then for a creator?

—Stephen W. Hawking

↪ KABBALAH SHOWS US one way of conceiving of creation and the development of the universe, including divinity. The new physics, including cosmology and quantum theory, shows us another. Each is appropriate to its time. Each can be a path to fuller mystical experience in our time.

Both can help us find answers to the questions:

❀ How did the universe get here?
❀ What is the role of humans in the universe?
❀ What is the relationship of humans to one another, to other beings, and to Earth?
❀ What is the relationship of humans to the divine?
❀ What is the relationship of the divine to the universe?

Kabbalah gives a metaphorical answer that on some level may be literal. The new physics gives a literal answer that on some level may be metaphor.

During the twentieth century, scientists intensified their quest to understand the origin and nature of the universe. This quest has been a journey leading away from what I term God the Manipulator and towards explanations that are consistent with many of the beliefs of ancient (and modern!) Goddess-centered spirituality—or what I call Goddess the Process. For the picture emerging from the "new physics" is that of an organic interactive web of a universe where change is a constant and unpredictability a given.

Patriarchal religions are unable to assimilate this new scientific knowledge, leaving those of their adherents who are scientifically knowledgeable to either choose between religious beliefs and scientific beliefs or live a kind of a double life: espousing God the Manipulator beliefs while at worship and investigating a universe that works just fine without manipulation when on the job.

In contrast, one of the most exciting—and least explored—aspects of Goddess spirituality is that many of the ancient concepts are confirmed by contemporary science, providing a way for this spirituality to grow to perfect fusion with science.

To understand how this is possible, let's look at a few late-twentieth-century scientific concepts and how they echo Goddess spirituality concepts.

THE UNIVERSE: STARS AND SPIRALS

Spirituality that honors the Goddess is often called "Earth-centered." Though many of us understand this term to mean a spirituality that is rooted in the earth, that sees humanity as part of nature and therefore is concerned with ecology, it is useful to look at the origin of the term "Earth-centered."

The term was first applied to the cosmology of Ptolemy (Alexandria, about 130 C.E.) in which the Earth was said to be the center of universe. All the planets and our Sun, as well as all other stars, it was believed, orbited Earth. This belief fit in nicely with the religion of the times, which dictated that a male

God, separate from nature (and elevated above it!) had created Earth and all its creatures according to his will and continued to oversee the machinery's daily operations.

Today we know the universe behaves quite differently, and we are certainly aware that Earth is not its center. When we talk about Earth-centered spirituality or Earth religions today, we are more likely to have in mind our interdependence with Earth from an ecological perspective and spirituality that fosters closeness to Earth and its cycles. Yet we would do well to reexamine the term "Earth-centered" in light of its original meaning and our current intent.

Using the term "Earth-centered" to describe contemporary Goddess spirituality, may mean risking getting stuck—or having the appearance of being stuck—in the rut of past beliefs that are no longer relevant.

This very irrelevance may, in fact, be the attraction of "Earth religions" for some: a rebellion against or escape from a complicated technological society.

One woman in a workshop I gave said to me, "I know the universe is out there, but I have enough just thinking about myself and my own problems."

Another woman remarked, "I don't want to think about science. It's too complicated and I don't understand it. I just want to do some simple Earth rituals."

Certainly turning toward spirit is one way of finding help for our problems. And doing "simple Earth rituals" can be good for both us and our planet. But I believe that when taken to the extreme, such attitudes sell us and Goddess spirituality short. Women have been culturally inculcated to believe science is too much for them to handle—both intellectually and emotionally. Patriarchal religion has taught us that science and religion are incompatible. Neither of these notions is true. It is time to become conscious of how these notions hold us back and to reject them. For just as to deny the scientific knowledge that describes the macrocosmos and the microcosmos would be intellectually stifling, so to limit our spiritual focus to Earth is to limit our spiritual development.

We may, therefore, want to consider whether it might not be more appropriate to refer to what we now call Earth-centered spirituality as nature-centered, and its religions, nature religions. These terms include not only Earth, but also the rest of the cosmos.

The observable size of the universe is about 1,000,000,000,000,000,000,000,000 miles.[1] (This unfathomable number—one followed by twenty-four zeros—is called a septillion in the United States and a quadrillion in Britain.) The furthest distance we can see is about 10 billion light years away, since the universe is estimated to be 10 to 20 billion years old.[2] Scientists tell us the universe is expanding, has no center, and is best visualized as being flat. It is not known whether it has edges. Galaxies (groups of stars) appear in clusters throughout the universe. We call our home galaxy the Milky Way. Cosmologists sometimes refer to it as "the Galaxy."

The Milky Way is shaped like a double spiral, with each of its two arms spiraling out from its center. It is 90,000 to 100,000 light-years across (that is, it takes light 90,000 to 100,000 years to travel from one end to the other). In its arms, about 100 billion stars rotate around its center every 100 million years. Earth orbits an average size star near the inner edge of one of the spiral arms. It takes light from the far end of our galaxy about 70,000 light-years to reach Earth. About 70 percent of the galaxies in the universe are spiral galaxies.[3] The spiral is an important symbol in Goddess spirituality, representing the continuity of the life cycle, and this is only one of several instances where the use of that symbol is substantiated by modern science.

Earth is eight light-minutes from its star, the Sun. (It takes eight minutes for the light from the Sun to reach Earth.) The next nearest star, Proxima Centauri, is about 23 million miles or four light-years away from Earth.

Our sun and its planets were formed about 4 to 5 billion years ago from a cloud of gas. At first Earth was very hot and had no atmosphere. Earth cooled and its rocks emitted gases that formed an atmosphere not at all conducive to human life. In addition to containing what would be to us poisonous gases, the atmosphere lacked oxygen. Nevertheless, primitive forms of life began, probably in the oceans. These life-forms eventually began emitting oxygen and the atmosphere slowly changed to its present composition, enabling development of the forms of life presently found on Earth—including humans—all of which contain the double spiral of life scientists call DNA.

Before Edwin Hubble's discovery in 1929 that distant galaxies are moving away from ours, scientists thought it likely that the universe was static. After all, this fit in well with the worship of God the Manipulator, who had put everything into place, just where it belonged. But the movement of other galaxies away from ours meant that the universe must be expanding.

To illustrate the concept of an expanding universe, some scientists advise picturing a balloon before it's inflated, with dots (representing galaxies) on it. As the balloon is inflated, the dots move farther away from one another. But note there is no center that the galaxies are moving away from and the space (between the dots) is also expanding. Some scientists prefer to picture a piece of rubber sheeting that is pulled at its edges, since the universe is now conceived by many physicists as "flat." This means that it is neither "closed" (in which case the density of matter would halt expansion and the universe would recollapse) or "open" (in which the expansion of the universe would continue forever). In a flat universe, the expansion will slow down, but not stop—at least not for a very, very, very long time.[4] It is not known whether the universe has edges. If it does, we can't observe them because their light would be too distant to reach us.

The most widely accepted theory is that universe has been expanding since the "big bang," a name (replete with possibly unintended sexual imagery) given by (male) scientists to an event most of them agree occurred 10 to 20 billion years ago. The big bang resulted from a "singularity," a situation where everything—all matter, space, and time—was compressed into a very tiny speck, much smaller than the period at the end of this sentence. But unlike the nearly weightless punctuation, this speck was extremely dense. An explosion occurred suddenly, marking the beginning of matter/space/time. Expansion at this point was the fastest it has ever been; gravity has been slowing it down ever since. The current rate of expansion is estimated at 5 to 10 percent every billion years.

(This description of the big bang may seem much like the kabbalistic spark of first emanation, except that in kabbalistic phallic imagery, the spark hardens like an erection and overflows like ejaculation.)[5]

To better understand what happened at the singularity—and afterwards—we need to delve into relativity theory (which has to do with space, time, light, and gravity) and quantum physics (subatomic science). While considering this, it is important to note that some scientists, most notably Hawking, are investigating theories that would make the big bang singularity unnecessary to the creation of the universe.

OUT OF TIME

If you were in high school before the 1970s, you may remember your science teacher saying that only a few people in the world were intelligent enough to understand Albert

Einstein's equation: $E=mc^2$. Today this equation is understood by most college (if not high school) physics students and a good number of their elders. In fact, it's considered easy stuff compared with the more complicated equations (and explanations of reality) that physicists have come up with since. What happened? Did everyone suddenly get smarter? Probably not. The more likely explanation is that it took our comprehension (rather than our intellect) time to catch up with this concept because it was so new and because it required us to look at the universe in a way that seemed to conflict with common sense—with everyday experience and observation. In much the same way as new religious concepts such as the Goddess are "unbelievable" when presented to a society that worships a patriarchal male god, Einstein's theory of relativity conflicted with our cultural conditioning.

Simply stated, $E=mc^2$ states a relationship between energy(E), mass(m), and light (c). Energy is equal to the mass of an object, times the speed of light squared. Light travels at 186,000 miles a second (or, stated another way, one meter per 0.000000003335640952 of a second.) It is impossible to go faster than the speed of light. To keep increasing its speed, an object needs more energy. For it to reach the speed of light, its mass must become infinite and then it can go no faster.

Einstein also showed that space and time are one unit. Physicists call this unit space-time. An example frequently given to explain this concept is that of a moving pulse of light (as from a lamp or flashlight) being flashed from the center of a moving train to both ends of the train at the same time. To a person observing on the train (who is moving at the same speed as the train) the light arrives at both ends of the train at the same time. But to someone observing from a stationary platform as the train passes, the light arrives at the front of the train before it arrives at the back.

Whose observation is correct? Both. On the train, the light is traveling equal distances. But viewed from the platform, the distance that the light has to travel to the front end of the train is shortened by the train's forward motion and the distance the light has to travel to the rear is lengthened. Therefore, the light arrives at the front before it arrives at the back. The speed of the light has not changed, but the distance it travels varies, depending on the location of the observer.

Space-time is a fourth dimension, and all events in physics are defined not only in the everyday dimensions of height, width, and depth, but in the space-time as well.

Here physics seems to verge into metaphysics. Physics tells us that what we experience in our everyday lives—that sense of past, present, and future—is not the ultimate reality. Some might even call it an illusion. Events appear to have a certain sequence because the speed of light is so much faster than any other speed. But in the reality of physics, past, present, and future are not absolutes but instead depend on the location of the observer in relation to the event.[6]

Does the relativity of space-time confirm experiences of what some Wiccans so appropriately call "starlight vision" or what others call "psychic"—a way of sensing or "seeing" that frequently comes with spiritual development, whatever the path, and which Goddess spirituality practices often incorporate?

In his general theory of relativity, Einstein further said that space-time is curved, due to the pull of gravity. Time appears to run faster out of Earth's gravitation pull, for example, because light is not slowed by gravity. Planets follow a straight path in curved space-time called a geodesic; Earth's orbit around the Sun appears to be an ellipse—that is egg-shaped—when viewed in only three dimensions. When the dimension of space-time is added, it is an elongated "helix" or spiral.

LIGHT CIRCLES AND CONES

Hawking describes the effect of a pulse of light in space-time as an expanding circle of ripples, similar to what occurs when you toss a stone into a pond. This pattern of light as it travels to the future through space-time is described as a cone. The tip, or small end of the cone is at the point at which the event—say a pulse of light—occurred. As the light travels through space-time the cone widens. Physicists call this the "future cone" of the event. (There is also a "past cone," which widens from the event to the past—the set of events from which a light was able to reach the present event.)

To those familiar with Wiccan practices, the similarity is startling. Witches—and many feminist spirituality groups which may not identify themselves as Wiccan—begin a ritual by casting a circle, which is often envisioned as a circle of protective light around the participants. Later in the ritual, the group "raises" (we might say develops, usually by chanting or dancing) what is called a "cone of power," envisioned literally as cone-shaped energy. And energy, as physics tells us, is light (and light energy).

For decades, theories about the nature of light varied. At first it was described as a particle. Then when scientists found that describing it as a particle didn't explain certain properties, it was said that light was actually a wave, a continuous surge of energy with peaks and troughs. Today, the most widely accepted theory is that light is made up of waves, but it behaves like particles; that both descriptions are necessary to fully understand light; and that one or the other may be more relevant, depending on what function we are examining.[7]

Light is emitted not in one continuous flow, but in packets of energy—specific quantities of light—called quanta (from which we get the term quantum physics). When it is described as a particle, a quanta of light is called a photon. Photons have no mass and travel at the speed of light. The lasers that we use in medicine, for light shows, and other purposes are essentially controlled and directed beams of photons.

When considered as waves, light occurs in different wavelengths. The color of light varies with its wavelength.

Wavelength is measured as the distance between one crest and the next and is sometimes referred to as frequency. Light we can see with the naked eye, visible light, is only a very small fraction of the entire light spectrum. The crests of visible light are between 40-millionths and 80-millionths of a centimeter. Light with wavelengths longer than visible light include radio waves (one meter or more between crests), microwaves (a few centimeters) and infrared (about 1/10,000th of a centimeter). Light with wavelengths shorter than visible light include ultraviolet, x-rays, and gamma rays, cosmic rays. (The closer the universe is toward red light, the colder it is and the older the source. The closer to blue, the hotter it is and the more recent the source.) Most of the light—the energy—in the universe then, can be seen only with the help of special technology. It nonetheless affects us. How appropriate, then, is the aim of many participants in Goddess spirituality to become sensitive to both the seen and unseen energy in the universe.

It is also easy to understand why light, the observable energy of the universe, is often a metaphor for immanent and encompassing divinity. Its changing quality is similar to shapeshifting—an attribute of the Goddess. Those of us who image divinity as both Goddess and God might want to see the wave aspect of light as representing the flow of the Goddess, and the particle aspect as representing the energy of the God. They are literally one in the light.

However, as we will see shortly, "light" is by no means the only component of the universe. And the image of the powerful "dark" aspect of the Goddess—which is no less divine than the "light"—is well supported by current physics theories.

Quantum Physics: The Subatomic World

Our understanding of the macroscopic universe is interwoven with our understanding of the subatomic world, since the universe is an expanded subatomic world.

In Goddess spirituality, rituals invoking (calling) the four directions with the corresponding "four elements" of earth, air, fire, and water as part of "casting a circle" has become common.

But what exactly do we mean by four elements? What is the origin of this concept?

Empedocles (fifth century B.C.E.) is generally credited with being the first to propose that all the matter in the universe is composed of earth, air, fire, and water. Aristotle (384-322 B.C.E.) continued this teaching and added a fifth element, "aether," which was "scarcely material in form."[8] He believed that matter could be continually broken down ad infinitum without coming to a piece of matter that could not be further divided. (As we have seen, some of these concepts were incorporated into kabbalistic thought.)

Another theory of the same time, not as widely accepted as the one Aristotle taught, was that of the Greek "atomists," who said that the Aristotelian elements could be broken down further into atoms (atom means indivisible in Greek), but that these atoms were the basic building blocks of matter and could not be further broken down.[9] As a corollary, they specified that matter was separate from spirit, which manifested as manipulative type deities (mostly male gods—by then the female goddesses had lost their power).

Around 2,000 years later, Isaac Newton stated in his theory of gravity that basic building blocks, as well as the forces between them, were created by "God" and could not be analyzed further because the universe was governed, like a machine, by immutable laws.

Today we know that air, fire, water, and earth are not basic elements and that neither the atomists' view nor Newton's theories hold at the subatomic level. While we may choose to keep the symbols of earth, water, air, and fire in our rituals for poetic purposes, the new physics, which so well substantiates long-held Goddess beliefs, may be a source of other, more up-to-date symbols.

DANCE OF THE PARTICLES

Despite what you may have been taught in school, we now know that the atom is not like a miniature solar system with electrons orbiting its nucleus much as planets orbit the Sun. Nor are protons, neutrons and electrons "elementary particles" or "basic building blocks."

In the late 1960s scientists began colliding (or in the vernacular, smashing) protons with other protons or electrons at high speeds. These experiments showed there are even smaller particles. These particles were dubbed "quarks" by researcher Murray Gell-Man from a quote in James Joyce's *Finnegans Wake*: "Three quarks for Master Mark." Joyce's three "quarks" were the local pronunciation of quart (as in beer); the physicists' three quarks are components of protons and neutrons. Quarks come in six types sometimes called "flavors" (which no one's ever tasted) and possess properties or qualities called "colors" (which no one's ever seen). The naturally occurring flavors in protons and neutrons are called "up" and "down." Another natural quark flavor called "strange" occurs in particles called "kaons."[10] The others—charmed, bottom and top—are human-made. A proton has two up quarks and one down quark. A neutron has two down quarks and one up quark. Holding these quarks together are messenger particles, which have been named, appropriately, "gluons."[11]

Solidity and separateness of matter are illusions in quantum physics.[12] As in Goddess spirituality, all is a related, interactive whole.

Although there appear to be no basic elements or building blocks, physicists talk about four types of "force-carrying" particles or "fields." Those of us in feminist spirituality might prefer to call them "flows."

They are:

—Gravity: The weakest, but most universal, it has the longest range. It always attracts (never repulses) and has no charge. It affects large objects much more than small ones. Its particle is the graviton.

—Electromagnetism: Much stronger than gravity and the second strongest of the four, it acts over shorter distances than gravity and affects smaller matter more than larger objects. It interacts with charged particles (for example electrons and quarks) and can have two kinds of charge: positive (+) or negative (-). (According to physicist Lawrence Krauss, the labels "positive" and "negative" are "arbitrary conventions" since you could call positive negative and vice versa and still have the same result.)[13] Electromagnetism can either attract or repulse, like the polar ends of a battery, with ++ and - - being repulsive and +-being attractive. The attraction is pictured as being caused by the exchange of its particles or photons.

—Weak interaction: Responsible for radioactivity, it powers the Sun and other stars and mediates neutron decay. In addition to virtual photons, particles that are weakly interactive are called "massive vector bosons" and are designated W+, W-, and Z^0. (This field is also called "weak nuclear.")

—Strong interaction: The strongest field, it holds quarks together in the neutron and proton and holds protons and neutrons together in the atom's nucleus. Its particle is the gluon. (This field is also called "strong nuclear.")[14]

How innovative, how appropriate it would be if Goddess spirituality groups added to the invocation of the four ancient "elements," these fields and added their symbols to altars.

I suggest the following correspondences:

Gravity (symbols: globe, planet)
⊗ Direction: North
⊗ Element: Earth

Electromagnetism (symbols: magnet, battery)
⊗ Direction: East
⊗ Element: Air

Weak interaction (symbols: sun, star, x-ray negative)
⊗ Direction: South
⊗ Element: Fire

Strong interaction (symbols: paste [flour and water], glue)
⊗ Direction: West
⊗ Element: Water

All but gravity can presently be unified, at least in theory. Scientists working on unified field theory believe all four fields will eventually be shown to be different aspects of one single field. We would call this one field—this one flow—Goddess, recalling her ancient epithet: "She who flows through all."

All particles have a property physicists call "spin," which is a way of describing what particles look like from different directions. There are four different types of spin: 0, 1, 2 and 1/2. These descriptions of spin are drawn from Hawking:

⊗ Spin 0 particle looks like a dot, the same from every direction.
⊗ Spin 1 particle looks like an arrow, different from different directions, but the same if you turn it 360 degrees.

⊛ Spin 2 particle looks like a line with an arrow on
each end; it looks the same if you turn it 180 degrees.
⊛ Spin 1/2 particle looks the same if you turn it twice.
Spin 1/2 particles make up matter; spin 0, 1, and 2
particles are responsible for the forces (or fields or
flows) between matter particles. (These last three
types of particles are called "virtual particles" be
cause they cannot be directly detected but have a
measurable effect. However, sometimes they do
exist as "real" particles, appearing as waves.)

Might we someday in our rituals have a "dance of the particles" in which some participants stand still, some turn all the
way around, others turn halfway around, and the rest turn
around twice?

In *The Tao of Physics*, Fritjof Capra describes the subatomic
world this way:

"Subatomic particles are dynamic patterns which have a
space aspect and a time aspect. Their space aspect makes them
appear as objects with a certain mass, their time aspect as pro-
cesses, involving equivalent energy. . . . Atoms consist of particles, and these particles are not made of any material stuff.
When we observe them, we never see any substance; what we
observe are dynamic patterns continually changing into one
another—a continuous dance of energy."

In *The Matter Myth*, Paul Davies and John Gribbin describe
matter as a: "network of interacting particles. . . . In some
sense the entire Universe can be regarded as a single quantum
system."

How well these dovetail with explanations of Goddess-centered spirituality, such as Starhawk's in *The Spiral Dance*:

"The primary principle of magic is connection. The Universe is a fluid, ever-changing energy pattern, not a collection
of fixed and separate things. What affects one thing affects, in

some way, all things. All is interwoven into the continuous fabric of being."

Scientists have found that this is literally true at the sub-atomic level: once two particles have interacted, no matter how far they may go from one another, they stay linked in some way, as if part of some invisible network. Scientists call this phenomenon "nonlocality."[15]

In the mid-1980s, scientists hypothesized that particles can be pictured as waves traveling on string, much like a spider on a web. This string has length but no other dimension. Known as string theory, this concept will only work if there are ten or twenty-six dimensions rather than the known four.

Another phenomenon on the quantum level has led scientists to generalize to the entire universe: you cannot be certain of both a particle's location and a particle's velocity at the same time. The act of measuring one changes the other. First formulated by Werner Heisenberg in 1926, this observation is known as the Uncertainty Principle and is accepted by physicists as a fundamental property of the universe.

The ramifications of this principle together with other quantum theories are described by Capra: ". . .nature does not show us any isolated 'basic building blocks', but rather appears as a complicated web or relations between various parts of the whole. These relations always include the observer in an essential way."

Since where each particle is at any given moment and how fast it's traveling cannot be accurately measured, it follows that the future cannot be predicted with any certainty. Scientists can only give likelihoods—or what they call "probabilities." Quantum mechanics, a branch of physics, takes as its scientific base that particles do not have separate, well-defined, observable locations and speeds. Instead they have a "quantum state," which is a combination of speed and location. Rather than a single outcome, a number of possibilities and the likelihood of each is predicted.

The theory of relativity showed that time was relative, actually part of a unit called space-time, and this meant that the distinction between past, present, and future did not exist apart from our perception of it. How, then, do scientists reconcile this with the uncertainty principle? The answer is that they haven't—yet. But they're working on it! In the meantime, perhaps this is a subject for spiritual investigation and interpretation.

One metaphysical possibility (probability?) is to understand that relativity theory tells us that "now" is relative and affirms the ability, through spiritual work, to move back and forth through time on a psychic level. Quantum theory tells us the future holds many possibilities, that some are more likely than others, and that the individual helps determine (or helps change) the future. These might be reconciled, at least on a metaphysical level, by saying that although past, present, and future may all be accessible to us, what we do in the present interacts with the future and can change it.

THE UNSEEN: DARK MATTER, BLACK HOLES, AND THE VOID

What we've discussed so far is what might be called the "seen"—or at least theoretically seen or observable—matter in the universe. But there is a whole other category that we might call the "unseen" and that physicists call "dark matter."

Physicists say that observable matter, including all planets and stars, all atoms and quarks, account for only a small amount of the material content of the universe. What is visible in the universe, or matter that emits light, accounts for at most 10 percent of the matter (or mass) of the universe. If the universe is "flat," then there is likely 100 times more dark matter than visible matter.[16]

One reason scientists have come to this conclusion is that the pull of gravity in the universe is so much greater than what seen matter can account for. According to Davies and Gribbin, nobody is sure what "this invisible stuff" is, but the best guess is that it's the "unseen residue of exotic subatomic particles left over from the big bang." Other authors offer other theories.[17]

Dark matter is not only out in the cosmos, it is in your room—indeed it is among all atoms and subatomic particles. These unseen "particles" interact with seen matter, but so weakly that we can't detect them. Scientists cite evidence that "some unseen influence" is at work from observing the way galaxies are distributed in space and noting certain irregularities.

Might we call this "unseen force" Goddess? Dark matter could be identified with the womb of the Mother, continually gestating particles, suns, galaxies, which flow from her in a continual stream of light. Dark matter might also be represented as the Crone aspect of the Goddess—dark and powerful. This seems especially valid in either a "closed" or "flat" universe, in which scientists say the combined gravity of the unseen "matter" may someday cause the "big crunch," the collapse and end of the universe.

The Crone image is appropriate, too, when we consider "black holes," which may account for a portion of the dark matter according to some theories. When very large stars (or sometimes entire galaxies) run out of fuel they collapse. As the star or entire galaxy shrinks, its gravitational field gets stronger, bending light cones increasingly inward and making it difficult for light, which in this case shifts toward red (as the temperature cools), to escape. Eventually no light—or any matter—can escape. A black hole will suck in any matter that gets within its field of gravity. (According to Hawking, who has done much of the basic research, black holes are actually "white hot" with x-rays and gamma rays emitting about 10,000 megawatts of energy. They appear black because none of this light is escaping.) At its complete collapse, the star becomes smaller than the smallest pinpoint, a singularity. Although no light can be seen from this singularity, it continues to exert gravitational pull.[18]

Scientists have identified several quasars (an abbreviation for quasi-stellar objects), regions of a galaxy that are shifting towards red and may be collapsing into black holes. In the spring of 1994, the first black hole was verified by the Hubble Space Telescope.

Physicists believe black holes are likely to outnumber visible stars, the mass of which is insufficient, for example, to explain the rotation rate of the Milky Way galaxy.

On the subatomic level, the mystery of the unseen is also best exemplified by the vacuum or void, which, as it turns out, is anything but empty. Instead it is teeming with the birth and death of "virtual" particles. The fluctuating energy in a vacuum causes the spontaneous appearance—the creation—of particles that exist only fleetingly before disappearing. This process is going on all the time in what we consider to be empty space around us—in the space between atoms of matter. The effects of these virtual particles upon "real" matter have been detected in many experiments. On the quantum level there is, then, a constant process of creation and an effect of the unseen on the seen.

Particles appear out of nothingness and return to nothingness. Except that sometimes, they may not return—at least not right away.

Scientists believe that if enough energy is available, virtual particles can become real particles. One theory of the origin of the universe, called the "inflationary theory," proposes just such a scenario: there was a void, a vacuum, and a virtual particle appeared. Rather than fade quickly away like other vir-

tual particles, it received enough energy to become a real particle. And virtual space-time was similarly promoted to real
space-time. The force needed to promote such energy (or "excitement" as it is called) in a vacuum would have to be a negative gravity force, called "antigravity." Such a force would make
space-time expand, explode, rapidly. As Davies and Gribbin
describe it:

"A tiny bubble of spacetime pops spontaneously and ghost-
like into existence as a result of quantum fluctuations, whereupon inflation seizes it and it swells to macroscopic dimensions.
Freeze-out then occurs and the expansion drops amid a burst
of heat. The heat energy and gravitational energy of expanding space then produce matter, and the whole assemblage
gradually cools and decelerates to the conditions we observe
today."

If this model is right, then the universe is flat and will ultimately (but not for a long, long, long, long time) collapse in
the "big crunch" and return to the void.

Hawking, however, offers an alternative. In addition to
eliminating the end of the universe, his proposal also effectively does away with a need for a "creator," or at least one that
is seen as existing outside (and before) the created. He says
it's possible for "spacetime to be finite in extent and yet to
have no singularities that formed a boundary or edge." This
means that there would have been no singularity at which the
laws of science broke down, no edge of space-time which necessitated a manipulative God or new laws. "The universe. . .would
neither be created nor destroyed. It would just BE." (Caps
his.) Hawking says that all the "complicated structures" of the
universe that seem to defy coincidence and call for some type
of conscious creator with a definite goal in mind, might be
explained by the unbounded universe together with the uncertainty principle.

The theory Hawking proposes, as his quote beginning this chapter suggests, is inconsistent with God the Manipulator.

But where does it leave Goddess the Process? In ancient mythology, the void was a Goddess—some called her "Vac"—from (or in) which life spontaneously arose. In this traditional concept of Goddess, she is not outside of her creation. She is one with it. She is Creation. She and the creation are one. Therefore, it makes little difference whether the universe simply is or whether it came into being; either way, the Goddess is the Universe. The universe's coming into being would not call for some deity other than Goddess to create it, for she would be present in the singularity; she would be the singularity and all that followed.

The lack of a singularity poses no problem for Goddess spirituality, since the concept of Goddess is the "being" of the universe rather than its manipulation.

If there was a singularity, then the Goddess was manifest at the singularity and continues to be manifestly immanent in the universe. And if there was no singularity, then the eternal yet ever-changing Goddess existed always, as she exists now and will continue to exist, though not necessarily in the same form. Like the universe in which she is immanent, the Goddess simply is—and continues to become.

The universe is infused with interactive, ever-changing energy manifest as light, but also present as dark. We call this energy—both seen and unseen, the light and the dark—Goddess. Through meditation and ritual we align ourselves to consciously interact with this energy.

In Goddess spirituality, divinity is both immanent and encompassing: Immanent in that the divinity flows through all matter, flows through us individually; encompassing in that all matter (and all people) flow in an interconnected web. This encompassing quality is part of what we called in the first chapter, "synergy." Goddess not only exists within us individually, but also infuses the entire universe. The network we form is greater than each part or person, yet influences each of us. In this synergy, the whole is greater than the sum of the parts, but there is no transcendent divinity that exists apart from it, no a priori cause that is separate from the universe.

Goddess spirituality is consistent with the abstractions of modern science and it also has the capacity, through personification of divinity, to speak to our concrete everyday experience and respond to our very human needs. Personification of divinity as female is necessary for political reasons, as has been said, to counter the persistently male image of "God." But it's needed for several other reasons as well. First, there is something in humans that wants to personify. Whether this can be explained by referring to Jungian archetypes or some other way, this need is real. If you doubt it, observe how we name hurricanes and seem uncomfortable using computers without trying to humanize them with cutesy names and friendly interactions (including the sound of the human voice).

In addition, aligning ourselves with the spiritual flow of the universe cannot be done solely through the intellect. This flow can best be reached when our emotions are aroused. Personification enables people to become emotionally involved with divinity, to experience a personal relationship with it (wouldn't it feel better to say Her?), and attain spiritual alignment; or participation in the spiritual flow.

We, therefore, choose the most appropriate personification. Both history and science affirm that this personification is most appropriately female. We may call her Goddess, Great Mother, Mighty Maiden, Wise Crone, or any of hundreds of names, ancient or recent.

How exiting it is that at a time when the concept of Goddess—interactive creative energy—has reemerged in social context and spiritual consciousness, scientific knowledge has outmoded the concept of God the Manipulator. For the new physics verifies and expands the words of a traditional Goddess song: "She is the weaver and we are the web." Quantum physics shows us it is also true that we are the weavers and she is the web. "She changes everything she touches," and everything we touch changes.

We are participants in an interactive reality we call the universe; we are participants in an interactive divinity we call the Goddess.

This glorious congruence is indeed a miracle—one worthy of celebration.

Waning Crescent Moon Ritual

The waning crescent moon, a time of great mystery, is rarely marked by rituals. So it is an appropriate time to create a ritual that incorporates insights from the new physics.

The group is gathered around the altar which has traditional symbols of the four directions along with those suggested earlier in this chapter, such as a magnet for east, a sun for south, paste for west, and a globe for north. Directions are called and circle cast according to the group's custom.

Here is the calling of directions given in chapter 1 with physics symbolism added. It is an example of how to incorporate physics references with traditional material. The physics references are italicized so the reader can easily see what has been added, but the words should be spoken the same as the rest. Purification is accomplished before the ritual begins, as is the custom of the group.

Calling of Directions

We honor the East
Home of air
Magnetic Messenger
March wind
Morning's song
Swift exchange
Eagle's flight
Aurora's breath *bringing light*
Welcome East

We honor the South
Home of fire
Radioactive field
Noon sun
Revealer of our inner selves
Flame of change
Heat of passion
Pele's power to destroy and to heal
Welcome South

We honor the West
Home of water
Quark glue
River's flow
Font of feelings
World's womb
Interactive bond
Kwan Yin's love *in matter manifest*
Welcome West

We honor the North
Home of earth
Gravity's gown

Root of life
Planet's path
Shaded mystery
Ground of being
Gaia's growth *and homeward tug*
Welcome North.

Waning Moon Invocation

On the wings of the waning moon,
we see the spiral arms of our galaxy,
and you, Goddess, are there.
On the wings of the waning moon,
we sense the spiral within us,
and you, Goddess, are there.
In the smallest of particles, you shine.
In waves of light, you flow.
In the dying of the darkest hole,
you bear the spark of new life.

Slowly fading crescent,
Honored Crone of change
Ancient One of transition,
open our minds to your wisdom
and our hearts to your love.
On the wings of the waning moon,
be with us here now.
So be it.

Guided Meditation

Seated comfortably, feet on floor, close your eyes, breathe
deeply, and relax. Let your breathing become slow, deep, easy.
Relax and continue breathing deeply and gently as. . .

You become aware of the darkness that surrounds you. Some might call this darkness a void; some might call it a vacuum; others might call it the womb of the Goddess, the womb of space-time.

You float gently now in this womb, float easily in this vast ocean of darkness.

And as you continue floating, you become aware that though you can *see* nothing around you, you can *sense* energy— a low level of energy—in this darkness and you realize that what surrounds you is not really empty, but—like the universe, like the ocean, like the womb—full of life. Take a moment now to sense the swirling energy that surrounds you in the dark.

(Pause)

And now let the energy swirl, let it spiral, until it gives birth to a speck of light.

(Pause)

Focus on that speck—that spark—and watch it grow.

It grows quickly now, expanding to fill our circle and to surround us. Take a moment now to experience the intensity of the light, experience its energizing power as it swirls in the center, experience its protection as it encircles us and glows above us and below us; shining all around us. (Pause)

Let the light fill your consciousness, fill the universe, until it becomes all that is. (Pause)

Now, in an instant, the immense light—in a flash—becomes many smaller lights, with one light shimmering before each one of us. Focus now on the light, the size of a candle flame, shining in front of you. (Pause) Slowly bring the light into your body in a way that is comfortable for you. (Maybe through one of your chakras: at your crown, or at your solar plexus. Or any other way that is comfortable for you.) As the light flows into your body, it grows in energy, bringing healing to every part of your body. Take a moment now to experience this energy, as the light flows through every part of your body. (Long pause of at least one minute)

Now become conscious of yourself as being filled with light. And as you envision this, you can see the light as infinitesimally small particles, shimmering in your body like a pointillist painting. And as you watch the shimmering particles, they begin to move together until they become waves—waves of energy, waves of light.

And now focus on one of these waves of light and, in a way that is comfortable for you, send this wave of light to one of the people sitting on either side of you and watch the light wave as it travels from you to this person. As you send the light, affirm that it is healing and brings blessings with it. At the same time, realize that others may be extending light to you and know that you can choose whether to receive it or send it back to its source.

As you watch the wave of light travel from you, see if you can notice: Does the person receive it?

(Pause)

Can you sense light being sent to you?

(Pause)

Now focus again on the light within you and this time send a wave of light out from you to the center of our circle. (Pause) See the waves of light coming from each of us into the center of the circle. Do they have color? Are they all the same? Different?

(Pause)

See now how the individual waves we each send into the center interweave and flow together, until the light pulsates and glows. And we are each attached to this pulsating, glowing center light by the wave we have sent from us. And now we can bring to us, through our individual light wave, energy from the center light. To help us do this, take a gentle but deep breath, and feel the energy flowing from the center through your light wave to you in the exact measure you require. And as you do this, you are strengthened and the center light also is strengthened, pulsating even more brightly. (Pause)

And when you have received the energy you need in the precise amount in which you need it, bring the light wave connecting you to the center back within your body in a way that is comfortable for you. (Pause)

And the light within each of us remains bright and energizing as we observe that the center of the circle is now dark. You observe the darkness now, sensing, knowing, that it is still pulsating with life. And as you focus on this pulsating void, if you wish, you receive from the void, from Vac, a message of wisdom—a message from the Ancient One who is with us now. This message may be for you, or for someone else here tonight, to whom you will transmit this message.

(Long pause)

And now you give thanks for the energy and wisdom you have received. And know that the light and the dark are both blessed, for she who flows through all is manifest in both.

And now, as you come back to this place and time, you bring with you both the energy and wisdom you have received.

Now move your body. Open your eyes. Come back to this place and time.

Song: "Mother of All"

(Suggested music: 2nd theme from 2nd movement of Mozart's Piano Concerto, No. 23.)

(1)

You are life's bright blaze and spark,
Spinning in quasar and quark,
Designing death's sacred shawl
Birth us
Bless us
Mother of all

(2)

Streaking the sky with your light,
Stroking the earth with your night,
Winter, spring, summer and fall
Calm us
Cheer us
Mother of all

(3)

You are the ebb and the flow,
Love's fire and sweet afterglow,
Elder's wisdom, child's scrawl
Teach us
Touch us
Mother of all.

(4)

Strengthen our hearts for your race
Suture our wounds with your grace
Incline your ear to our call
Hold us
Heal us
Mother of all.

Sharing of Response to Guided Meditation

Participants can now share what they experienced in the guided meditation, including what they felt as they sent light waves to others and others sent light waves to them, what they felt as they sent light to the center and drew energy from the center, and what messages they received from the void.

Dance

The movements of this dance are borrowed from traditional Hungarian women's dances. The special handhold, called a "front basket," weaves the group together. In this dance, the weaving symbolizes the interdependence of the universe. It is achieved by extending your arms out to the sides until you grasp the hands of the person on the other side of the person on your left and the person on the other side of the person on your right. (Don't cross your arms or hands in front of you!) The dance moves to the left. In a step known as a "down rita," the right foot is placed slightly in front of the left and you shift your weight gently forward on the right and back on the left as you move to the left. The dance can be done to music or simply to rhythm instruments. In either case, the rhythm should go well with the step. It can be moderately slow throughout or can begin slow, get faster for a short time, and then slow down for a while near the end.

(Alternately, the group can create a "dance of the particles" described on page 166.)

Blessing

Ancient One, thank you for being with us.
May the cycle be complete.
May ancient wisdom inform the newest science.
May the light of new knowledge illumine the spirit.
May waning flow into waxing.
May the old become new.
So be it.

(The circle is open according to the group's custom.
Food is shared.)

Endnotes

INTRODUCTION

1. Helen Diner, *Mothers and Amazons*, The Julian Press, 1965; Esther Harding, M.D., *Women's Mysteries*, Longmans, Green and Co., 1935 (republished by Harper & Row, 1976).

2. Riane Eisler, *The Chalice and the Blade*, Harper & Row, 1987; Marija Gimbutus, *Goddess and Gods of Old Europe*, University of California Press, 1982; Merlin Stone, *When God Was A Woman*, Harcourt Brace Jovanovich, 1976; Starhawk, *The Spiral Dance*, Harper & Row, 1979; Rosemary Radford Ruether, *Women-Church*, Harper & Row, 1985; Mary Daly, *Gyn/Ecology*, Beacon Press, 1978; Naomi Goldberg, *The Changing of the Gods*, Beacon Press, 1979.

3. Starhawk, *The Spiral Dance*; Margot Adler, *Drawing Down the Moon*, Viking Press, 1979 and Beacon Press, 1981.

4. Z. Budapest, *The Holy Book of Women's Mysteries*, Susan B. Anthony, Coven No. 1, 1979.

5. Ruether, *Women-Church*.

6. Carol P. Christ, "Why Women Need the Goddess" in *Womanspirit Rising*, Carol P. Christ and Judith Plaskow, eds., Harper & Row, 1979.

7. Blu Greenberg, *On Women and Judaism*, The Jewish Publication Society of America, 1981.

8. Lynn Gottleib, *She Who Dwells Within*, Harper SanFrancisco, 1995.

CHAPTER 1

1. Riane Eisler, *The Chalice and the Blade,* Harper & Row, 1987.

2. Barbara G. Walker, *Women's Rituals,* Harper & Row, 1990, p. 105.

3. Mary Daly, *Beyond God the Father,* Beacon Press, 1973, and *Gyn/Ecology,* Beacon Press, 1978.

4. Dion Fortune, *The Mystical Qabalah,* England, 1935; republished, Samuel Weiser, Inc., 1984 and 1993, p. 242.

5. Eisler, *The Chalice and the Blade.*

6. Ibid.

CHAPTER 2

1. Raphael Patai, *The Hebrew Goddess,* third enlarged edition, Wayne State University Press, 1990, pp. 26-27.

2. Translation, Daniel C. Matt, *The Essential Kabbalah,* Harper San Francisco, 1995, p. 209.

3. Elliot R. Wolfson, *Circle in the Square,* State University of New York Press, 1995, pp. 13, 16, 20-22. Wolfson also points out that in this androcentric symbolism, the scroll's crown corresponds to the corona of the penis, symbolizing that the feminine divine has become part of the male deity, rather than remaining independently divine.

4. Matt, *The Essential Kabbalah,* p.3.

5. Patai, *The Hebrew Goddess,* p. 74.

6. Gershom Scholem, *Kabbalah,* Meridian, 1978, p. 9.

7. Ibid. p. 15.

8. Ibid. pp. 13, 16.

9. Ibid. p. 21.

10. Matt, *The Essential Kabbalah,* p. 76 and explanation, pp. 187-188.

11. Patai, *The Hebrew Goddess,* p. 99.

12. Scholem, *Kabbalah,* pp. 23-24.

13. Patai, *The Hebrew Goddess,* p. 111.

14. Scholem, *Kabbalah*, pp. 99, 312.

15. Matt, *The Essential Kabbalah*, pp. 5, 105.

16. Ibid. p. 6.

17. Ibid. p. 50.

18. Perle Epstein, *Kabbalah: The Way of the Jewish Mystic*, Shambhala, 1988, p. 57.

19. Matt, *The Essential Kabbalah*, pp. 7-10.

20. Epstein, *Kabbalah: The Way of the Jewish Mystic*, p. 47.

21. Wolfson, *Circle in the Square*, pp. 68, 69, 74, 77.

22. Matt, *The Essential Kabbalah*, p. 52; interpretation, p. 176.

23. Scholem, *Kabbalah*, pp. 227-228.

24. Matt, *The Essential Kabbalah*, pp. 80, 135.

25. Epstein, *Kabbalah*, p. 46, and Wolfson, *Circle in the Square*, pp. 9-28. Elliot Wolfson explains that in early Kabbalah, Torah was understood to be wholly feminine and synonymous with Shekinah. Beginning with the *Zohar* and continuing for several centuries, various teachers attempted to assert that written Torah (and especially the scroll) was male, however, the female imagery of Torah kept reappearing, especially in the Hassidic tradition.

26. Matt, *The Essential Kabbalah*, p. 140, interpretation, p. 211.

27. Patai, *The Hebrew Goddess*, pp. 114-116.

28. Ibid. p. 117.

29. Ibid. p. 129.

30. Ibid. p. 133.

31. Ibid. pp. 158-160.

32. Ibid. p. 249.

33. "The Hypostasis of the Archons," trans. Bentley Layton, in *The Nag Hammadi Library, 3rd edition*, ed. James M. Robinson, Harper Collins, 1990, p. 167.

34. Patai, *The Hebrew Goddess*, pp. 39-43.

CHAPTER 3

1. Raphael Patai, *The Hebrew Goddess*, third enlarged edition, Wayne State University Press, 1990, p. 270.

2. Ibid. pp. 270-273.

3. J. Ben Shlomo in Gershom Scholem, *Kabbalah*, Meridian, 1978, p. 401.

4. Translation, Daniel C. Matt, *The Essential Kabbalah*, HarperSanFrancisco, 1995, p. 24.

5. Gershom Scholem, *Kabbalah*, Meridian, 1978, pp. 93-94.

6. Matt, *The Essential Kabbalah*, p. 39.

7. Patai, *The Hebrew Goddess*, p. 167.

8. According to Wolfson, all powerful female traits become male in Kabbalah, so that when breasts lactate, they become phallic, the milk identified with ejaculate overflow. See Elliot R. Wolfson, *Circle in the Square*, State University of New York Press, 1995, p. 109.

9. Patai, *The Hebrew Goddess*, p. 171. For a thought-provoking discussion of the derivation of the godnames Yahweh and Adonai, see Sigmund Freud, *Moses and Monotheism*, Alfred A. Knopf, Inc. 1939.

10. Matt, *The Essential Kabbalah*, p. 41.

11. Ibid. pp. 30-39.

12. Ibid. pp. 40-43.

13. Ibid. pp. 40-45.

14. Ibid. pp. 43-46.

15. Ibid. p. 49.

16. Ibid. p. 160, explanation, p. 217.

17. Scholem, *Kabbalah*, pp. 128-129.

18. Matt, *The Essential Kabbalah*, p. 94.

19. Ibid. p. 28.

20. Scholem, *Kabbalah*, p. 130.

21. Wolfson, *Circle in the Square*, p. 105.

22. Matt, *The Essential Kabbalah*, pp. 94-95.

23. Wolfson, *Circle in the Square*, p. 66.
24. Scholem, *Kabbalah*, pp. 137-139.
25. Ibid. p. 138.
26. Ibid. pp. 139-140.
27. Ibid. p. 141.
28. Patai, *The Hebrew Goddess*, p. 275.
29. Scholem, *Kabbalah*, p. 142.
30. Patai, *The Hebrew Goddess*, p. 166.
31. Wolfson, *Circle in the Square*, p. 91.
32. "The Gospel of Thomas," translated by Thomas O. Lambdin, in *The Nag Hammadi Library, 3rd edition*, ed. James M. Robinson, Harper Collins, 1990, p. 138.
33. Matt, *The Essential Kabbalah*, p. 122.

CHAPTER 4
1. R.G. Torrens, *The Secret Rituals of the Golden Dawn*, Samuel Weiser Inc., 1973, p. 219.
2. Mary K. Greer, *Women of the Golden Dawn*, Park Street Press, 1995.
3. Most Golden Dawn members used the Italian deck called "Tarocco Italiano." However, two of the most commonly used decks today, known as the Rider-Waite and Thoth decks, were created by Golden Dawn members. The Rider-Waite deck gets its name from the publisher of the deck, Rider and A.E. Waite, who helped the artist, Pamela Coleman Smith, with ideas for the art. However, apparently his instructions influenced Coleman Smith's portrayal of only the major arcana (twenty-two key cards) of the deck. The illustrations on the cards of the four suits (wands, swords, cups, pentacles)—the first Tarot minor arcana to be fully illustrated—are most likely entirely the creation of Coleman Smith, who was active in the women's suffrage movement. (See Greer, pp. 405-409.) The deck therefore should rightfully bear Coleman Smith's name, at the very

least in conjunction with Waite's. Her initials appear on each card in serpentine lettering that is so much part of the design as to be almost unnoticeable.

The Thoth deck is the creation of idea man Aleister Crowley and artist Lady Freida Harris. Its name derives from the Egyptian name for the equivalent of the gods Hermes or Mercury, which could be said to be the "patron gods" of the Golden Dawn, which was also known as the Hermetic Order of the Golden Dawn.

4. Torrens, *Secret Rituals of the Golden Dawn*, p. 28 and Greer, *Women of the Golden Dawn*, p. 263.

5. Eliphas Levi, *The Book of Splendours*, Samuel Weiser, Inc., 1973, pp. 59-60.

6. Levi, *The Book of Splendours*, p. 131.

7. Torrens, *Secret Rituals of the Golden Dawn*, pp. 15, 212.

8. Greer, *Women of the Golden Dawn*, pp. 165-178.

9. Ibid. p. 59.

10. Torrens, *Secret Rituals of the Golden Dawn*, pp. 42, 220, 231.

11. Greer, *Women of the Golden Dawn*, p. 59.

12. Torrens, *Secret Rituals of the Golden Dawn*, pp. 77-78.

13. Ibid. pp. 75, 106.

14. Ibid. pp. 156, 158, 176-177.

15. Ibid. p. 200.

16. Ibid. p. 41.

17. Ibid. pp. 36, 42.

18. Ibid. p. 201.

19. Ibid. p. 189.

20. Ibid. pp. 162, 188.

21. This reversal is reminiscent of, and may be derived from, the Lurianic blaming of the cosmic catastrophe on the (female) vessels for not being able to contain (male) emanations.

22. Torrens, *Secret Rituals of the Golden Dawn*, p. 130.

23. Ibid. pp. 161-2, 161, 285.

24. Ibid. pp. 173-174, 251, 270.

25. Ibid. p. 25.

26. Greer, *Women of the Golden Dawn*, pp. 350, 452.

27. Dion Fortune, *The Mystical Qabalah*, first published in England,1935; reprinted by Samuel Weiser Inc., 1993, pp. 2, 60, 73.

28. Ibid. pp. 110-112.

29. Ibid. p. 51.

30. Ibid. pp. 124, 144.

31. Ibid. p. 151.

32. Ibid. pp. 162-165, 189-204.

33. Ibid. pp. 218-241.

34. Ibid. pp. 253-254, 267.

35. Ibid. pp. 283-287, 485.

36. Greer, *Women of the Golden Dawn*, pp. 163, 220.

37. Fortune, *The Mystical Qabalah*, pp. 149-152.

38. Ibid. pp. 127, 155.

39. Ibid. pp. 298-300.

40. Fortune, *The Mystical Qabalah*, pp. 105-265; and Pamela Eakins, *Tarot of the Spirit*, Samuel Weiser Inc., 1992.

41. Fortune, *The Mystical Qabalah*, p. 107.

42. Ibid. pp. 55-56.

CHAPTER 5

1. Raphael Patai, *The Hebrew Goddess*, third enlarged edition, Wayne State University Press, 1990, pp. 137-151.

2. Gershom Scholem, *On Kabbalah and Its Symbolism*, Schocken Books, 1965, pp. 100, 143.

3. Judith Plaskow, *Standing Again at Sinai*, HarperSanFrancisco, 1990, pp. 6-10; and Patai, *The Hebrew Goddess*, p. 107.

4. Gershom Scholem, *Kabbalah*, Meridian, 1978, p. 25.

5. Although, as previously mentioned, the feminine noun Ru'ah was originally used for this sefirah, for this initial analy-

sis, we are using what has come to be the most commonly used Hebrew noun.

6. Scholem, *Kabbalah*, p. 137.

CHAPTER 6

1. Stephen W. Hawking, *A Brief History of Time*, Bantam, 1988, p. 10.

2. Lawrence M. Krauss, *The Fifth Essence: The Search for Dark Matter in the Universe*, Basic Books, 1989, pp. 54, 194.

3. Ibid. p. 67.

4. Ibid. p. 100.

5. Elliot R. Wolfson, *Circle in the Square*, State University of New York Press, 1995, p. 61.

6. Michael Talbot, *The Holographic Universe*, Harper Perennial, 1991, p.41

7. John Gribbin, *In Search of Schrodinger's Cat: Quantum Physics and Reality*, Bantam Books, 1984, pp. 82-85; and Talbot, *The Holographic Universe*, p. 34.

8. Krauss, *The Fifth Essence*, pp. 10-12.

9. Hawking, *A Brief History of Time*, p. 63.

10. Krauss, *The Fifth Essence*, p. 228.

11. Hawking, *A Brief History of Time*, p. 65.

12. Paul Davies and John Gribbin, *The Matter Myth*, Simon and Schuster, 1992, p. 224; and Fritjof Capra, *The Tao of Physics*, Bantam, 1976 and 1994.

13. Krauss, *The Fifth Essence*, p. 222.

14. Hawking, *A Brief History of Time*, pp. 69-74; and Krauss, *The Fifth Essence*, p. 228.

15. Davies and Gribbin, *The Matter Myth*, p. 224.

16. Krauss, *The Fifth Essence*, pp. 158, 195.

17. Ibid. pp. 163-249.

18. Hawking, *A Brief History of Time*, pp. 99-113.

About the Author

Judith Laura has been involved in Goddess spirituality since the late 1970s, when her first rituals were published in the journal *WomanSpirit.* She is author of the book *She Lives! The Return of Our Great Mother* (Crossing Press, 1989).

Laura's rituals, articles, and poetry have appeared in *SageWoman, Voices of Women, Broomstick,* and *Pudding Magazine.* She lives in the Washington, DC, area and teaches workshops and classes on Goddess spirituality.